Praise for
Armor of God

"*Armor of God* is just the resource I'm looking for as a mom of two tweens. Full of conversation-starting questions, bonding activities, and practical ways to put what we're learning together into action, this book equipped me to help my kids face the very real war before them. Working through this resource, I (for the first time in a long time) found myself helping my daughters get dressed—this time with holy, kingdom-forged armor."

—**JL Gerhardt,** author and minister

"I loved every chapter of this book! My favorite chapter in *Armor of God* is 'The Shield of Faith.' Being a single mom, 'faith over . . .' became my mantra, and I said it over and over again when I needed a gentle reminder of God's promises to me. I loved Catherine reminding me that the Shield of Faith is not something we wear; rather, we use it to cover ourselves from evil and trust God's love for us no matter what we are going through. My faith can move mountains!"

—**Dede Babcock Johnson,** St. Dunstan's Episcopal Church, boy mom

"Parents and ministry leaders alike will be blessed by this work. As a father, I love the idea of using this text as a tool in equipping my fourth grader with the armor of God as he prepares to enter middle school. As a veteran student ministry pastor, I appreciate how this tool equips parents for their role of discipleship, but also lends itself for use in a ministry context. The suggested activities in the text, as well as the 'Letters from the Battlefield,' illustrate clearly the immediate and long-term application for the armor of God in the life of both student and adult. Enjoy this special journey with the tween in your life!"

—**Lucas Randall,** family ministry student director, Hill Country Bible Church

"As a parent of five, I can attest to the spiritual warfare plaguing our nation's youth. *Armor of God* is just the fortification our family needs to help fight the battle. I am looking forward to sharing Cat's thoughts and insights with not just my teenage sons, but also with the rest of my children and their friends. We need all the reinforcements we can get!"

—**Erica Jones,** mom of five

"As an adult, it is difficult navigating the battlefield in our lives, our world. Additionally, we are given the responsibility of teaching our children how to overcome the obstacles in their lives. Satan preys on weakness; it is crucial that we are equipped in faith to face the battles we encounter. This book is a must-have in the home and ministry of the church!"

—**Jodi Marfell,** director of children's ministry, Bethany United Methodist Church, Austin, TX

"My son is ten years old and in fifth grade. As he matures and crosses all of life's bridges, I'm grateful to have a toolkit with specific examples of prayers and activities that address challenges faced by youth today. When we read this book together, we not only strengthen our relationship with each other, we grow in our faith."

—**Julie Long,** busy working mom with a preteen boy, Spring Hill, TN

ARMOR OF GOD

ARMOR OF GOD

A BIBLE STUDY
for Tweens and Parents in Today's Spiritual Battle

CATHERINE BIRD

Foreword by Teri Lynne Underwood

LEAFWOOD
PUBLISHERS
an imprint of Abilene Christian University Press

ARMOR OF GOD
A Bible Study for Tweens and Parents in Today's Spiritual Battle

LEAFWOOD
P U B L I S H E R S
an imprint of Abilene Christian University Press

LIBRARY OF CONGRESS CATALOGING-IN-PUBLICATION DATA
Names: Bird, Catherine, 1976– author.
Title: Armor of God : a Bible study for tweens and parents in today's spiritual battle / Catherine Bird.
Description: Abilene, Texas : Leafwood Publishers, 2021. | Includes bibliographical references.
Identifiers: LCCN 2020029983 (print) | LCCN 2020029984 (ebook) | ISBN 9781684261611 (paperback) |
  ISBN 9781684269471 (ebook)
Subjects: LCSH: Spiritual warfare—Biblical teaching—Textbooks. | Parents—Religious life—Biblical teaching—
Textbooks. | Children—Religious life—Biblical teaching—Textbooks. | Parent and child—Religious aspects—
Christianity—Textbooks.
Classification: LCC BV4509.5 .B546 2021 (print) | LCC BV4509.5 (ebook) | DDC 235/.4—dc23
LC record available at https://lccn.loc.gov/2020029983
LC ebook record available at https://lccn.loc.gov/2020029984

Cover design by Bruce Gore | Interior text design by Sandy Armstrong, Strong Design

The map of Turkey on page 30 was adapted from https://commons.wikimedia.org/wiki/File:Turkey_map2.svg#file, author Thomas Steiner.

Leafwood Publishers is an imprint of Abilene Christian University Press

ACU Box 29138 | Abilene, Texas 79699

1-877-816-4455 | www.leafwoodpublishers.com

21 22 23 24 25 26 27 / 7 6 5 4 3 2 1

For Dr. Bill Robertson Jr. and all the soldiers he trained
and encouraged in God's army.

Well done, good and faithful servant.

CONTENTS

ACKNOWLEDGMENTS

Boy, howdy . . . this has been a season of battle *for sure*. My agent and I joked that writing about spiritual warfare was not for the faint of heart, and I don't think we really understood how right we were. The enemy was determined to keep this Bible study from seeing the light of day, but that assignment failed. I may be tired and bruised from battle, but so are those who have stood valiantly with me throughout the development of this book. I am here to tell you we are stronger with our people. God did not design us to battle alone, and thank goodness for that.

My husband is living proof that our God is loving and kind. In all the ways I imagined my Prince Charming, I could never have put together a package as awesome as Travis Bird. He makes me laugh. He holds me when I cry. Then he makes me laugh again. He even watches Hallmark. Growing older with him has been such a fun adventure, and I can't wait to see where God leads us next. Travis Bird is my rock-solid partner in life, my baby daddy, and my best friend. In the crazy writing seasons, he tosses chocolate toward my desk and tackles just about every Pinterest project I can dream up. Seldom does he complain, and frequently does he champion our family. I love happily-ever-afters, but my very favorite love story is ours. I love you, Travis Bird.

I am honored that I get to do life with some pretty amazing people. My bestie, KMcD, and I have served on the spiritual battlefield together since first meeting at Texas A&M University many, many, *many* moons ago. We have lived much life together. Our sisterhood is full of laughter, tears, births, deaths, major milestones, all the space in between, and no small number of Sonic runs. Friendships like ours are precious because friendships like ours are so very rare. She and her hubby (#2!) have stood in the gap for my family more times than I can count, just as we have stood for them. They are the family we choose. While Travis Bird throws chocolate, my bestie brings my favorite writing candle whenever I run out, a daily beverage to keep the juices flowing, and runs carpool like a champ! This book might have happened without her, but it wouldn't have been pretty. Thank you, sister. I love you.

The Tribe—I love my tribe, y'all. My prayer for each person reading this book is that you have a tribe of your own. Truly. Until my mom's devastating illness, I did not fully appreciate the importance of community or how God is reflected there. Above all, the Bible says we are to love one another. *The Tribe*, as we call our close-knit group of friends, does this so well. Life is tough. And let's be honest—sometimes the enemy scores a hit and knocks us off our feet and flat on our face. Getting off the ground is so much easier when someone extends their hand to help you. We do not live life perfectly, but we do live life together. We show up for one another. We have grace. We choose to be present. #mcbirdfritzclassicalhomeschoolacademyforever

I'll always be Daddy's girl. He was the first man I ever loved. In my heart, he's still that strong guy in army fatigues who scooped me up often to tell me how much he loved me. Thank you, Daddy, for loving me so well and for the gift of fun. Not every girl has the best blend of Tim the Toolman Taylor and Clark Griswold as their dad. You're my hero. I love you to the moon and back!

I miss my mama. She's having a big ole party in heaven, and I wouldn't wish her back into her broken earthly body for anything. I miss her, though. Yet God has been so faithful to raise up other mamas to love me—mamas who make me feel special on my birthday, mamas who pray for me on the tough days and celebrate with me on the awesome ones. Mama #2 (or *Ghee* as she is to my babies), Aunt Debbie, Ms. Bonnie . . . thank you. I love you!

SK, my cousin and the sister of my heart, I am always grateful for you. No one makes me laugh harder. Fearless, funny, and full of words of wisdom, I can always count on you to bring a smile to my face. Know how much you are loved! Now pack your bags. Dollywood awaits!

LP, I know Jesus lets Foxy Roxie and Sandy Sue peek down here from time to time, and I know how proud they both are. So thankful for you and the sisterhood we share. #buceesorbust

Prayer warriors, and there are many, thank you. From the bottom of my heart, thank you for standing with me throughout this writing season. I know many of you took some tough hits, but you stood firm and continued to battle alongside me. I am forever thankful for each and every one of you.

A Note to Parents

Armor of God is an eight-week study designed and intentionally written for tween kids (approximately ages nine to twelve) to share with their mom or dad—or both! As parents, we can probably all agree that raising children in today's culture is not for the faint of heart. There is a spiritual war raging around us, and the enemy prowls around our camp like a roaring lion and seeks to devour our children (1 Pet. 5:8). We are called as parents to equip our children and teach them the ways of the Word so they do not become casualties to the ways of the world. The Bible tells us to clothe ourselves with the armor of God (Eph. 6:14–19) to defend against the enemy and his schemes.

That is the heart behind this study. It is chock full of wisdom and practical modern-day examples that explain what the spiritual war is, who we are fighting against, and how and why we have a winning strategy through Jesus. By the end of this study, I pray parents and tweens will understand that Satan's attacks come in many forms (depression, anxiety, bullying, cheating, lying, and more). Yet, with the armor of God, they can stand firm against evil and resist the enemy's schemes to separate them from the One who created them and loves them most.

Format of the Study

This study is unique in that each chapter is not broken down into daily reading and study. This is an eight-week format designed to facilitate joint

Bible study and discussion between parents and their tweens. Parents and kids may approach weekly study however it fits into their schedules. If you want to read and study a little bit each day, great! If it works better for you to consolidate into two days, go for it. The structure of this study is intentionally flexible.

SITREP Sections

SITREP is a military term for *situation report* and within the context of this study provides readers with a status check and understanding of the current topic of discussion. There are a few ways to approach the SITREP sections within this study, which include conversation starters and questions to get you thinking more deeply about each chapter discussion. Answer the questions in each chapter together or on your own. Some parents and tweens may choose to write directly in the Bible study book, while others may prefer a notebook or journal where you can jot down your thoughts separately. In the pilot group, the girls were definitely preferential to journals while the boys preferred talking through their thoughts aloud in a group setting. Choose whatever method works best for you and your family. If you are going through this study with a group, your facilitator will lead you through some engaging discussions and fun activities that relate to each week's topic.

Parent and Tween Activities

In this study, you will also find activities specifically designed for parents and tweens to complete together each week. These activities are meant to facilitate fellowship between parents and kids while helping them dig a little deeper into the biblical topic of each chapter. The activities presented throughout the study focus on designing and constructing each reader's own "spiritual" armor, which in a biblical context reflects the elements of armor historically worn by Roman soldiers. During the first week, tweens and their parents will draft a rough concept for their own designs. At the end of the study, tweens and parents will don their fancy new armor and engage in an entertaining battle of their own. The pilot group used colored powders, but any messy, fun substance will do! Have fun and feel free to include other family members. This can be an exciting adventure, so enjoy and get started today! (*Note this adapts well to small group study.*)

Letters from the Battlefield

I am most excited about this new Bible study feature. Sometimes, my friends and I lament how our children seem deaf to the sound of their parents' voices. We lend a piece of advice, and it simply goes in one ear and out the other. However, a peer of said child could lend the same advice and the words are taken to heart. While we know as parents we weren't alive when the dinosaurs roamed the earth, we *have* traveled quite a bit more on the road of life than our mini-mes. In addition to the wisdom of their *elderly* parents, it is helpful for our children to hear from peers about their own struggles, which may seem more relatable than our "Well, when I was your age . . . ."

That's not to say that the parental wisdom we impart isn't important and relevant, because it is. It is also just as critical for kids of today to hear from other tweens and teens who are battling similar struggles or have already weathered really rough seas and have insight to share as a result of those experiences. These are teens and tweens who have been active on the spiritual battlefield and who have been brave enough to share their stories with you and your children. These tidbits are included at the end of each chapter and are aptly called "Letters from the Battlefield." I pray your children are touched and inspired by the vulnerability of these young men and women and that your tweens heed the call to equip themselves with the armor of God.

Let's get started!

A NOTE TO TWEENS

Dear Friend,

Welcome to Spiritual Warfare 101, tween edition! I'm so happy you're here, and I know we're going to get through this together! As a teen myself (you'll be there soon too!), I experience spiritual warfare on the daily in every aspect of my life. Whether it's through peer pressure, a whisper in my ear, or even a testing situation, it's everywhere. So, let's dive right in and dig a little deeper into this thing called spiritual warfare!

First of all, I feel the toughest spiritual warfare I fight against comes in the form of peer pressure. It's so easy to listen to your friends and want to fit in. Trust me. I've been there. Most of the time it's harmless, innocent fun . . . *until* it's not. Whether people are urging you to gossip, try drugs or alcohol, or perform an act you know does not honor God, sometimes it's hard to say no, especially when it's your friends.

You know that gut feeling you get when you know you shouldn't be doing something? Yeah, that's the one. Wanna hear a secret? That's the Holy Spirit! The Holy Spirit is constantly watching over you and helps you combat spiritual warfare and the enemy. I know I've been in many situations like this—and when I listen to the Holy Spirit, it turns out great! I try to live my life for God and choose to make right decisions that honor him, but sometimes it doesn't work out that way. *Sometimes*, I choose to ignore that gut feeling from the Holy Spirit and make a choice that doesn't quite honor God, and I face the consequences for that choice. But even though I may have lost that single battle, I did not lose the war, because I have the best tool at my side, ready to help combat anything that comes at me. Thanks, Holy Spirit! So, learn to listen to that gut feeling, because the Holy Spirit knows what he's talking about!

Spiritual warfare and the enemy come in many, many forms. The enemy is always one step behind, whispering in your ear. Maybe it's to cheat on the math test you didn't study for (guilty!); or maybe it's skipping church to go hang out with friends instead. The enemy is extremely sneaky, and he has many tricks up his sleeve. But don't worry! Remember, you've got the Holy Spirit on your side. In these situations, I like to combat spiritual warfare with simple logic, such as, "I can always do corrections if I fail this math test or just do better on the next test," or "I can hang out with my friends after church today." I use these simple statements and logic because I like to pretend Jesus is standing right next to me, watching me, and listening to me (because he always is!). I like to pretend he's there physically. If Jesus was standing next to you, you probably would make the decision to best honor him, right? Me too! Spiritual warfare has got nothing on us with Jesus by our side!

Now y'all, pay attention to this next sentence. The enemy hits us the hardest, and we have the biggest struggle with spiritual warfare, when it comes to who we are and who God says we are. The enemy *loves* to whisper lies in our ears when we mess up. He may say things like, "Wow, no way *you* can be a child of God; you make *way* too many mistakes," or "Hmmm, you look really ugly today; actually you look awful every day." I have struggled with this, and I still do on a daily basis. The enemy makes up sneaky lies that get into our heads; and the sad part is, sometimes we start to believe them. But God doesn't want us to believe those lies! He wants us to believe we are fearfully and wonderfully made in his image (which is pretty awesome to me)! Yet, I totally understand the struggle. The best way I have found to remember that I am created in the image of God is to write and stick a note on the mirror I look at every day, telling myself how much God loves me and how worthy I am to him. This helps so much when I'm feeling down or letting the enemy sneak into my head and my heart.

Here's another fun fact about spiritual warfare: the enemy loves to kick us when we're down. Gross, right? We are most susceptible to listening and believing what the enemy has to say if we're already in a bad place. But don't fret! There's a quick and easy way to combat the enemy and win more battles when he attacks! Ask God to protect your heart and your mind from the enemy. Proclaim that you know you are a beautiful or handsome child of God and that you are fearfully and wonderfully made in his image. Now this may take some practice; it definitely took me a couple tries. But I promise, Jesus is always on your side; he will be the first to protect your heart with all his might. Spoiler alert!!! Jesus *always* wins.

So my last piece of advice is this: Use your God-given armor (Eph. 6:14–18) to protect your mind and your heart. Know that God is just a quick prayer away and is always on your team to combat the enemy and his evil tricks. Every single time. You've got this, friend!

Abby F.

FOREWORD

About a week ago, my daughter turned twenty. And a couple of days ago, I visited a brand-new baby, born in the same hospital where our girl was born. My husband and I walked past the room where Casiday made her grand entrance into the world and headed into the room where a tiny little boy, just a few hours old, was nestled in his mother's arms. And I thought how true that old saying is: "The days are long, but the years are short."

You're in one of the hardest seasons. The tween years are tough on parents and on tweens. Everyone is learning to navigate life as it seems to change almost every day. It can feel completely overwhelming. And, if we aren't careful, we can easily find ourselves in what seems like a battlefield in the one place that is supposed to be a refuge—our homes.

In these pages, you'll find that the very best way to minimize the battle is to keep our eyes on the *real* battle for our hearts. Paul says our enemy isn't flesh and blood but rulers and powers in this world (Eph. 6:12). We have to know the truth about this and understand that we need to fight for our relationships, not against each other.

Once we recognize the real enemy, we need to make sure we're using the right tools. And that's where this amazing resource comes in. You'll spend the next several weeks learning about the spiritual armor that God has given to each of us. As you learn what each piece offers and how to best use it, you'll also discover how remembering that we're on the same side helps us encourage and support each other, even when it's hard.

If you haven't considered doing this study with a group of other parents and tweens, can I just whisper a word of encouragement for you to think about that? While our homes are our first community, the additional insight and support we gain from learning and applying God's Word together is another layer of protection and strength. The enemy will work hard to separate you from your people, but know that your community is essential in battling against Satan in the spiritual war.

Cat and I have done some serious prayer battle together. We've held each other up and stood in the gap for one another and our families many times. Through those experiences (and countless phone conversations full of laughter and tears), we've discovered the beauty of fighting with our community for the things that matter most. Your community makes you stronger. Now is a great time for you to learn those same truths.

You'll also want to pay careful attention to the "Letters from the Battlefield." Let's face it: I'm old. Cat is old. And you probably think your parents are old. (We know you are way too polite to say it, but we also know there's a reason "Okay, boomer" is such a popular saying.) It might be easy for you to dismiss what we're saying or even tuck it away, thinking it will be good information for you when you're old one day. These letters, which appear in each chapter, are from people just a few years ahead of you—young men and women who have grown up with cell phones and the pressures of social media. They know more about the way the battle can rage in your life than your parents or other adults may understand. I hope you'll pay careful attention to what they've shared and that you find encouragement through their words of wisdom. (Parents, you might be surprised at how much their words can encourage and challenge you as well.)

Y'all, Cat Bird is one of my dearest friends. She has a heart bigger than her Texas home. She loves God and his Word, and these pages are evidence of how much she wants you to know the same Jesus who has changed her life. I'm grateful for the way she loves and encourages me, and I really believe you're going to feel that same deep care she has for you as you dig into *Armor of God*.

I love what Cat has created in this study. We can impact both those long days and the short years in a powerful way when we spend time together—parents and sons/daughters—in the Word. You're holding a tool that can help you grow closer together and grow closer to the Lord.

As you work through these pages, you'll learn new things about one another and become a source of encouragement to each other as you focus on fighting the battle we all face. Enjoy these moments you have, and be certain that your time in the Word and the time you invest in your relationship will reap big rewards!

Praying for you all!
Teri Lynne

Teri Lynne Underwood is a pastor's wife and future nurse's mom. She lives in north Alabama, where she teaches Bible study, speaks at women's events, does lots of laundry, and wrangles her family's very grumpy basset hound, Buddy. She's the author of *Praying for Girls: Asking God for the Things They Need Most* and has contributed to several books and devotionals, as well as the *(in)courage Devotional Bible*. You can connect with Teri Lynne on Instagram at @terilynneu or on her website www.TeriLynneUnderwood.com.

Stand, therefore,

with TRUTH LIKE A *belt* around your waist,

RIGHTEOUSNESS LIKE *armor* on your

chest, and your feet *sandaled* with *readiness* for

the GOSPEL OF *peace*. *In every situation take up*

the SHIELD OF *faith* with which you can

extinguish all the flaming *arrows* of the evil one.

Take the HELMET OF *salvation* and the

SWORD OF THE *Spirit*—which is the

word of God. PRAY AT ALL *times* in the

SPIRIT with every *prayer* and *request*, and

STAY ALERT with all PERSEVERANCE

and INTERCESSION for all the *saints*.

Ephesians 6:14–18 (CSB)

PART ONE

Preparing for Battle

*For our struggle is not against flesh and blood,
but against the rulers, against the authorities,
against the cosmic powers of this darkness,
against evil, spiritual forces in the heavens.*

Ephesians 6:12 (CSB)

Chapter One

Knowing
Your Enemy

*For though we walk in the world, we do not fight according
to this world's rules of warfare. The weapons of the war we're
fighting are not of this world but are powered by God and effective
at tearing down the strongholds erected against His truth.*

2 Corinthians 10:3–4 (*The Voice*)

The Backstory

Last summer, my family and I took a trip to Washington, DC. We spent
ten very full days visiting historical landmarks, including the White House,
Mount Vernon, the Lincoln Memorial, several Smithsonian museums, and
a long list of other exciting sites within the National Mall and beyond. Each
destination was packed with middle-school children and their chaper-
ones taking in all the sights, sounds, and smells that make the US capital
such a memorable place. Of course, each fun stop was outfitted with a gift
shop where tourists could purchase some fun mementos to take home. In
addition to the gift shops, vendors lined the streets, offering all kinds of
interesting wares for passersby.

One day during our trip to DC, we were on a guided walking tour
through Ford's Theatre and nearby landmarks when our group passed by
the Trump International Hotel. We noticed the presence of police and
that traffic had been halted in both directions. It dawned on us that the
president was *inside* and about to depart for the White House. No matter
how you feel about the man personally, there is some exhilaration at seeing
the president of a nation—a sight which many people never see in their

lifetime. Cheering ensued as the president was rushed to the awaiting motorcade, and then several black vehicles sped by surprised spectators. The whole unexpected encounter lasted less than twenty minutes, but it was a highlight of our trip to the nation's capital and one of the first experiences our kids share when they talk about their trip.

I imagine this is how tourists felt in ancient Ephesus when they visited the renowned Temple of Artemis, which was built in honor of a goddess of fertility (also sometimes known as Diana). Once named as one of the Seven Wonders of the World and built in what today is western Turkey, the Temple of Artemis was undoubtedly a sight to behold when it stood proudly in its heyday, around the sixth century BC.[1] The temple was longer than a modern-day football field and stood surrounded by one hundred columns, each roughly fifty-five feet tall.[2]

As you can imagine, hundreds of thousands of tourists flocked to this destination each year in the ancient world—many to attend the annual month-long celebration honoring Artemis. Travelers would have spent money on lodging, food, souvenirs, and the same types of things we might purchase if we were vacationing away from home today. Ephesus was a bustling modern city in ancient times, much like Washington, DC, is for us today. If we were to stroll down the streets when the Apostle Paul visited in the spring of 52 AD, we would see a busy harbor with ships from all over the world docked at port and a busy marketplace full of vendors selling goods and services to visiting tourists.

Paul and his missionaries visited other important cities like Ephesus during the days of the early church. As Jesus asked Paul and the other disciples to do (Mark 16:15), Paul faithfully visited new places, often big cities like Rome, Ephesus, and Corinth, to start churches. While he was unable to stay in each place permanently, Paul wrote letters to the people he had visited to lend encouragement and wisdom as they continued the important work of growing Christian communities.

A Letter with Impact

When Paul was in Ephesus, many people accepted Jesus into their hearts and converted to Christianity. As more and more people became Christians, fewer people visited the Temple of Artemis and less became interested in purchasing souvenirs that represented a goddess they no longer worshipped. Eventually, this impacted the vendors in and around the temple, who made their living from the goods they sold. They were unhappy with Paul and his fellow missionaries and the effect their teachings had on the temple marketplace. Thus Paul had to pack up his suitcase and leave Ephesus, leaving the important work of growing the church that had been planted with new believers in Jesus Christ.

Paul's letter to the Ephesians was to remind them what it means to be part of the body of Christ and to encourage them as they faced opposition in the days of the early church. Belief in Jesus and following his teachings meant public persecution, and many Christians in those days met in secret (as some Christian communities around the world are still forced to do today). However, that is not the danger that Paul referenced in Ephesians 6:12. Within his letter about Christian living and responsibilities, Paul also wrote to the Ephesians about an *unseen* war—a battle waged between the spiritual forces of good and evil.

> For our struggle is not against flesh and blood, but against the rulers, against the authorities, against the cosmic powers of this darkness, against evil, spiritual forces in the heavens. (Eph. 6:12 CSB)

What Is the Unseen War?

Simply explained, "War can be defined as organized fighting, on a large scale, over a period of time between different ethnic, national or racial groups."[3] There have been a depressingly large number of wars throughout human history. The longest wars spanned centuries, while some recorded conflicts lasted only days. These wars represent many battles fought on a variety of fronts by different types of soldiers.

In the case of war, smaller battles ensue. While a commander in chief may direct the strategy of each conflict, the tactical objectives are executed by a hierarchy of soldiers. The *unseen* spiritual war Paul references in both Ephesians and 2 Corinthians can be explained in much the same way. While the first war in recorded history took place in Mesopotamia in c. 2700 BCE between Sumer and Elam,[4] the first spiritual battle took place long before:

> A battle broke out in heaven. Michael, along with his heavenly messengers, clashed against the dragon. The dragon and his messengers returned the fight, but they did not prevail and were defeated. As a result, there was no place left for them in heaven. So the great dragon, that ancient serpent who is called the devil and Satan, the deceiver of the whole world, was cast down to the earth along with his messengers. (Rev. 12:7–9 *The Voice*)

According to the Bible, Satan was given dominion on earth and mankind has been a target ever since. If we look back in Scripture, we learn Adam and Eve faced spiritual opposition in the Garden of Eden. Remember the serpent? Genesis 3 paints the picture of a crafty snake who tempted Eve into eating the forbidden fruit and, in turn, sharing the fruit with Adam. Prior to the first sin, Adam and Eve lived in community with God within what we can imagine was the most beautiful place on earth. They had much freedom, and Scripture tells us God only gave them a single restriction: do not eat *one* fruit. Yet they were tempted by the sight of such a delicious-looking fruit, and the serpent encouraged them to take what they wanted. Hmmm, sounds familiar, doesn't it?

Isn't this how spiritual opposition still translates to our lives today? How are we tempted into choices that seem appealing but are not necessarily good for us? Temptation takes many, many different forms. Some of us are tempted by electronics, social media, food, drugs, vaping, anxiety (yes, we can be tempted to give in to worry and fear), laziness, busyness . . . the list is endless. We'll unpack this idea further as we dig deeper into who our enemy is, how he preys on our weaknesses, and what we can use to defend against these attacks.

For now, it is important to understand that the spiritual war is real. It is happening all around us, even though we cannot see it. The purpose of this study is to help you become battle ready by understanding the landscape of the spiritual battlefield, familiarizing yourself with your armor, and learning how to defend against the enemy's attacks. The more you know, the better prepared you will be.

Most Importantly, You Are Never Alone

War is scary business, to be sure. Imagine being on a battlefield with no knowledge of your enemy and no one beside you to help you fight. A terrifying thought, right? Fortunately, that is not your situation. *You are never alone.*

Before we take a closer look at the enemy, let's take a closer look at ourselves. First and foremost, let's address what could be an elephant in the room and dispel any mistruths about *who* you are and *whose* you are. You are intentionally crafted by a loving God for an important purpose (Ps. 139:14, Eph. 2:10, Luke 12:7, Jer. 29:11). Every single one of us has doubted this truth—likely on more than one occasion. And guess what? That's part of the enemy's scheme to distract you from the truth of your royal lineage. You bear the image of our Creator (Gen. 1:27), crowned with honor and glory to accomplish important work while you are here on earth (Ps. 8:4–6, Heb. 2:5–7). *That* is who you are.

When you accepted Jesus into your heart and asked him to be your Lord and Savior, you experienced what Christians call a "spiritual rebirth" (2 Cor. 5:17). The covenant of the Old Testament in the Bible, which required a blood sacrifice for sins, was fulfilled by Jesus when he took our sins to the cross. He died so that we could have the gift of salvation and eternal life with our Father in heaven (Eph. 2:8). We didn't do anything to earn it. We actually don't deserve it, but God loves each and every one of us so much that he sent his one and only Son to bear the shame of our sins (John 3:16). The old covenant of laws and works was replaced by the new covenant of grace. Christian author Jack Zavada said, "Both the Old and New Testaments are the story of the same God, a God of love and mercy who gave his people the freedom to choose and who gives his people the opportunity to come back to him by choosing Jesus Christ."[5] The gospel is called the good news for a reason!

As part of God's family, Mark tells us we are to "go into all the world and preach the gospel to all creation" (Mark 16:15 NIV). That is our battle objective: to share the love of Jesus with everyone until the entire world has heard the good news (Matt. 24:14). It may seem daunting, but remember you are part of an army of Christian soldiers (1 Pet. 5:9). *You are not alone.*

Who Is the Enemy?

It is important to know our enemy, because he certainly knows you. When we, as Christians, refer to the enemy, we are referring to Satan, which comes from a Hebrew word meaning "adversary." Everything we need to know about the enemy we can find in Scripture. In a nutshell, Satan is J-E-A-L-O-U-S. He is blatantly envious of God and wants to take his place. Look up Isaiah 14:13–14 and complete the section below. (*Hint:* Use a Bible translation like the NIV that shows five "I will" statements.) It reveals how deeply jealous Satan is of God by the promise the enemy makes himself.

You said in your heart,
"I will _____;
I will _____;
I will _____.
I will _____;
I will _____."

Wow, Satan is so full of himself! He could not be more wrong.

You have probably seen scary depictions of the devil (another name we use for Satan, translated from the Greek word *diabolos*), where he looks like a dragon with horns or some other creepy creature from the underworld. The truth is our enemy is probably quite appealing on the outside, but he is definitely ugly on the inside. Much like the origin of the word *devil*, one of the enemy's signature qualities is his *diabolical* nature. While our objective is to spread the gospel to the ends of the earth, Satan's goal is to stop us. Make no mistake. The enemy is clever, strong, and relentless in his pursuit to wage war against the kingdom of heaven.

When Satan was exiled from heaven, God cast him down to the earth (Rev. 12:7–9), and he has dominion here (Luke 4:5–7). What exactly does that mean? It means that Satan is active among the realm of earth, and while he is extremely powerful, he does not have omnipotent control over humanity. He cannot hear our thoughts. We retain our free will, and once we become Christians, we can call upon the power of the Holy Spirit to resist him (Luke 10:19).

Our enemy never rests, never sleeps, and he is ruthless in his objective to stop the spread of the gospel. He's no dummy either. An effective commander has spies and patrols that help perform reconnaissance and collect valuable information on their enemy. Military forces all over the world and throughout the span of history have engaged the work of soldiers whose sole mission is to probe into the enemy's territory and use surveillance and patrols to learn more about them and their capabilities. What are their strengths? What are their weaknesses? The enemy has studied us, and he knows where we are vulnerable to attacks.

These attacks come in many forms. Writing this study, for example, placed me on the front lines of a fierce spiritual battle. The enemy is likely less than thrilled at the idea of new generations of Christian soldiers learning how to defend against his attacks. I believe there was an assignment issued to keep me from finishing this study for you. The enemy's attacks came in many forms: illness, an unexpected job change, a misunderstanding with a friend, a child hurting from a painful breakup with her boyfriend, a dog yacking on my brand-new rug, a global pandemic, and the list goes on. When I would sit down to focus and write, distractions would abound. If you are walking in the way of Jesus and chasing after him with abandon, spiritual attacks will happen to you, too. It is part of our walk as Christians. We will face trials and endure hardships the enemy places in our paths. However, we have hope.

Spoiler alert: The war has already been won. God is imminently more powerful than Satan. Good versus evil is not even an accurate comparison. Think of a gnat on the sun. When Jesus died on the cross, he took even more power away from Satan. Remember, our enemy is angry and jealous of God. Everything he does is to distract us from focusing on *what* and *who* matters most.

While the enemy can make our lives pretty miserable from time to time, he does not have the power or authority to separate you from God. Once you accept Jesus as your Lord and Savior, you are marked as Christ's own (Eph. 1:13). This means you become part of the body of Christ—a community of believers who affirm and encourage one another as we work toward the common goal of sharing the good news around the world. The "Letters from the Battlefield" included at the end of each chapter in this book provide further proof (and encouragement) from teen soldiers who are defending against spiritual opposition and actively engaged in the unseen war.

The Enemy's Aliases

Like the talented con artist he is, Satan has many aliases. Look up the following Scriptures and match each with Satan's corresponding name.

Ephesians 6:12	the tempter
Matthew 4:1	anointed cherub
Isaiah 14:12–14	the deceiver
Ezekiel 28:14	father of lies
Matthew 4:3	son of the morning
John 8:44	prince of darkness
Revelation 12:9	the devil

Preparing for Battle

In Ephesians 6:10–17, Paul explains the armor of God, which we as Christians can put on to defend against Satan's schemes. Why do you think he used the analogy of a Roman soldier?

Paul actually was not the first to use the illustration we find in Ephesians. If we flip back to the Old Testament to Isaiah 59:17, it says, "He put on righteousness as a breastplate, and a helmet of salvation on his head" (ESV). Paul's explanation of the armor of God points back to the Old Testament reference, but he develops the idea further by using a symbol that the Ephesians would have been very familiar with—the Roman soldier.

Ephesus was a Roman-governed city, and the Ephesians would have seen Roman soldiers every day. Paul used imagery that would have made sense to the Ephesians. As we dig further into our study of the armor of God, we will unpack each piece and examine its purpose more closely to understand why Paul's analogy is still relevant for Christians today.

An Activity for Parents and Tweens:
Personalizing Your Armor of God

The activities included throughout this entire study are focused on designing and constructing each participant's own armor of God. For week one, explore the following components of a Roman soldier's armor:

- Belt
- Sandals
- Helmet
- Breastplate
- Shield
- Sword

Spend some time talking through what you learn and draft a rough concept for your own designs. Each person should have their own! At the end of this study, tweens and parents will don their fancy new armor and engage in an entertaining battle. The pilot group used colored powders, but any messy, fun substance will do. Start thinking now, and get creative!

While parents and tweens are working on their armor designs, discuss what spiritual opposition looks like for each person. Take some time to pray over your designs and thank God for his provision of spiritual armor to defend against Satan's attacks. If you are unsure of what to pray, the following is a prayer offering you might consider.

> *Dear Father in Heaven,*
>
> *Thank you for crafting me with such love and purpose. I know you loved me so much that you sent your one and only Son to take the punishment for my sins. That love is so much more than I can comprehend, but I want to love more deeply. Show me how to love like you do, Lord.*
>
> *Help me as I prepare for spiritual battle with the enemy. Give me insight to learn all the intricacies of the special spiritual armor you have provided, Lord. Help me remember to suit up and protect me and those I love from the enemy's attacks. Send your angels to stand with me and help push the enemy back.*
>
> *Forgive me where I fail you, God. Please send your Holy Spirit to guide me, to instruct me, and to help me prepare for the important work you have called me to do. I am here, Lord! <YOUR NAME> here, reporting for duty!*
>
> *In Jesus's name, I pray,*
> *Amen.*

WHAT'S YOUR
SITREP?

It's time for a situation report, so let's check your understanding and dig deeper into the context of Chapter One.

1. Read Ephesians 6:10–19 together. Write below in your own words what Paul is trying to explain to the Ephesians.

2. Why do you think Paul used the analogy of a Roman soldier?

3. If you have time this week, do a little research on what the armor of Roman soldiers looked like. Compare those pieces to what we read about in Ephesians 6.

4. What is the unseen war, and are we defenseless? Why or why not?

5. Who do we need protection from in the unseen war?

6. How does the enemy tempt you into choices that do not honor the person God has designed you to be? What do you think the enemy sees as your weakness?

7. Do you think the armor of God is for physical protection or spiritual protection?

(Note to parents: Hopefully, this will open the door for you to talk about the need for spiritual protection. We'll unpack this further in future chapters and discuss scenarios we encounter in our daily lives that support the need for our God-given armor.)

8. Look up Colossians 2:15 and write it in the space below. Talk with your mom or dad about what this passage of Scripture means.

THIS WEEK'S **BATTLE PLAN**

*This is a weekly call to action based on the topic of each discussion.

1. Write out Ephesians 6:10–19. Personalize the passage and change it to first person. For example, "I will be strong in the Lord and in the strength of his might." *Battle tactic: We will dig into the sword of the Spirit, the Bible, in a later chapter, but just like a Roman soldier, it is important to be familiar with your weapon! The more comfortable you are with your weapon, the better equipped you will be to wield it against the enemy.*

2. Pray the armor of God over yourself and each member of your family each day this week.

Letters from the Battlefield

Dear Parents,

At the end of each chapter in my previous Bible studies, I included a letter from me to moms reading and working through those studies with their tweens. Much _life_ has happened since I wrote my last study, and I have prayed about how to make these times studying the Word of God more meaningful for readers. The truth is the older my children grow, the more their hearts are open to the words of their peers.

Peer influence is powerful. We don't always think of peer pressure as positive, but it can be a really, really good thing. Even as adults, we draw support and wisdom from our peers as we navigate the sometimes tumultuous path in front of us. The more I thought and prayed through plans for this study, the more I felt led to incorporate letters from older teens who might be able to lend encouragement to tweens who are participating in this study. Thus each chapter concludes with "Letters from the Battlefield," which I pray encourage you and your tweens, who may be facing a battle of their own. These letters are raw and vulnerable and paint a picture of what the spiritual battlefield looks like for our children today.

It seems like just yesterday I was listening to Tiffany on my Walkman and trying to look like Cyndi Lauper for picture day at school when, in reality, I probably looked more like Punky Brewster. Shockingly, our kids today don't relate as well to the social struggles we faced when we were their age. While the idea of slap bracelets has stood the test of time, today's youth has no idea how awesome Trapper Keepers were/are.

Yet the social challenges that surpass age gaps include mean girls, bullies, the temptation for whatever society says is the latest "it" thing. Atari's _Frogger_ may not hold a candle to Nintendo Switch's _Mario Kart_, but both can be considered huge _Time Bandits_. (_Ahem_. Eighties kids, you totally get what I just did there.)

In short, the teens of today are certainly facing scenarios we never could have imagined and vice versa. However, as parents, we still have important words of wisdom to share. My prayer is that tweens working through the pages of this study will open their hearts as they unpack knowledge of the unseen war and their own personal armor of God. I pray that your conversations are deep and meaningful. I pray that you and your children draw closer to one another while leaning more deeply into your relationship with God. I pray that none of you remains unchanged as you prepare to take your place on the spiritual battlefield.

Hugs,
Cat

Dear Friend,

This topic of spiritual opposition touches my heart, as my walk with God has never been easy. I'm sure that you maybe can feel the same way, as God can put you in situations that you never saw coming. There have been quite a few times in my life when I've tried to take my own path rather than his. It is in times like these that I try my best to remember that God has gone before me to create an entire plan for my life from beginning to end. This, most importantly, includes all of the good and bad in between.

As I grew up in the church, I oftentimes found that I couldn't wrap my mind around why God would decide to place battles in our life. Whenever something difficult would happen to me, I felt that it was as if he just decided to leave me all alone to deal with these awful circumstances by myself.

Just over a year ago, I was heading into my second year of high school with my sister, who was starting her senior year. I felt that everything was finally falling into place with my friendships and extracurricular activities—that was until my parents sat my sister and me down to tell us that my mom had been diagnosed with breast cancer. My world stopped, and I was left completely shocked by the news. I couldn't fathom why God would do this to someone so important to me, and I became very angry with him. I grew farther and farther apart from God, as I felt that this was his doing. I didn't want to go to church, read the Bible, or even pray to ask for help. I felt that I was stranded alone in the desert with no way to get out. This was _exactly_ what the enemy wanted.

This was my struggle until an army of people—friends, family, and loved ones—came to our rescue. They brought us meals, care packages for my mom, and offered rides for my sister and me. At first, I was reluctant to accept their help, as these were things my mom had always done for us. Over time, I gradually realized that God sent

these people to surround my family with love and support so that she could fight. These people were God's
army, and they were the hope that we needed for her to
continue on. For the first time in a while, I sat down to
pray and ask God to forgive me for distancing myself from
him. I went back to church and began to understand that
although he allowed for my mom to have cancer, he pur-
posefully handpicked this group of people to fight my
mom's battle right alongside her. I decided then that the
only way we were going to make it through this was by
keeping a strong and steady faith in him.

Through every treatment and surgery, my family prayed
that she was beating the cancer. Without our faith, this
journey would've been so much more difficult, as we
wouldn't have had God to lean on. The day she rang the
bell (signifying the end of her cancer treatment) was a
moment I'll never forget. I was beyond grateful that my
mom could say that she was a cancer survivor.

Through all of the pain I watched her go through, it
became very apparent to me that God sometimes has to
bring you to your worst in order to let you be your best.
I thought God had failed me, but instead, he showed up
in ways I had never have seen before. As hard as those
times may be, God surrounds you with an army to defeat
whatever battle, big or small, lies ahead. May you rest in
the knowledge that God is in control and trust that he
continues to walk right beside you wherever you go.

Blessings,
Abby J.

Dear Friend,

My name is Breck, and I am sixteen years old. I was born into a Christian family and accepted Christ as my Lord and Savior at a very young age. Even so, my relationship with God did not deepen significantly until the summer before my freshman year of high school, when I attended a church camp. It was then that I felt my relationship with God really grew. After this experience, I started to live my life for God and practice his ways. I am trying to grow in my relationship with him and act as the person I know God wants me to be, even though that can be tough as a teenager in this day and age. As I continue to grow in my faith, I have noticed many of the situations my friends and I are faced with now are actually encounters with spiritual opposition, which the Bible tells us to expect when we become Christians.

One of the ways the enemy distracts us in today's culture is by tempting teens to spend a lot of money on designer clothing, high-end electronics, and other non-essential items. I spend a lot of my own money on secondary things such as Uber Eats, Vans sneakers, and music. Although spending money on nonessentials can be totally okay, it seems to be done in excess among teens of our generation. This is one of the ways Satan tries to separate us from our faith in God. Many teens today focus on temporary desires and worldly items, rather than focusing on saving our money. As soon as money hits our hands, we are enticed to exchange it for some cool or trendy "thing" that society tells us we need right now. Worldly items like these can be distracting from

God and easily consume our lives. We need to be more cautious and try to resist Satan's temptations to over-indulge." Set your minds on things above, not on earthly things" (Col. 3:2 CSB).

The spiritual battlefield that we face every day is a place where every decision matters. It requires you to have the ability to make tough decisions, even if that means saving your birthday money rather than blowing it on an expensive new pair of shoes. The spiritual battlefield also requires us to encourage one another, not to grow jealous of what other teens have. This is tough, guys. It's hard sometimes to walk around school and avoid envying what other teens have. On the spiritual battlefield, Satan attacks us when we are weak and not expect-ing it. He sometimes attacks us through unexpected sources, such as through a close friend. His attacks are clever and calculated. He knows how to distract us. As Christians, spiritual opposition is not a matter of _if_; it is a matter of _when_ it will happen.

There is hope, though. When I am dealing with spiri-tual opposition, I go to my family or God for help. I try to focus on the big picture rather than my present and temporary desires. I defend against spiritual opposition with Scripture such as:

Do not love this world nor the things it offers you, for when you love the world, you do not have the love of the Father in you. For the world offers only a craving for physical pleasure, a craving for everything we see, and pride in our achievements and possessions. These are not from the Father, but are from this world. And this world is fading away, along with everything that people crave. But anyone who does what pleases God will live forever. (1 John 2:15-17 NLT)

Avoiding the temptation of worldly desires definitely is a struggle for all of us, but it is also an important part of Christianity. As Christians, we must try to understand that just because we desire something does not mean that we should have it. Teens nowadays particularly are constantly enticed with buying things for worldly reasons; this is an easy habit to have and a tough habit to stop, but we must try. Following Jesus requires the ability to make choices that go against what we might specifically want in the present and quite honestly against primarily what society says is good for us.

My hope is that we can be a generation that says "no" to the ways of the world and "yes" to the ways of God. I pray we can all plan for our future and avoid expensive worldly items and other nonessential temptations that are only temporary. Our hope in Jesus is never ending.

Sincerely,
Breck

NOTES

[1] "Temple of Artemis at Ephesus," *Turkish Archaeological News*, December 14, 2016, https://turkisharchaeonews.net/object/temple-artemis-ephesus.

[2] Larry Richards, *International Children's Bible Field Guide: Answering Kids' Questions from Genesis to Revelation* (Nashville: Tommy Nelson, 2006), 195.

[3] T. D. P. Dugdale-Pointon, "War," History of War, January 8, 2001, http://www.historyofwar.org/articles/concepts_war.html.

[4] Joshua J. Mark, "War in Ancient Times," *Ancient History Encyclopedia*, September 2, 2009, http://www.ancient.eu/war/.

[5] Jack Zavada, "Old Covenant versus New Covenant," Learn Religions, January 29, 2020, http://www.learnreligions.com/old-vs-new-covenant-700361.

PART TWO

Understanding Your Armor

Therefore take up the whole armor of God, that you may be able to withstand in the evil day, and having done all, to stand firm. Stand therefore, having fastened on the belt of truth, and having put on the breastplate of righteousness, and, as shoes for your feet, having put on the readiness given by the gospel of peace. In all circumstances take up the shield of faith, with which you can extinguish all the flaming darts of the evil one; and take the helmet of salvation, and the sword of the Spirit, which is the word of God.

Ephesians 6:13–17 (ESV)

Chapter Two

THE BELT
OF TRUTH

Assuming that you have heard about him and
were taught in him, as the truth is in Jesus.

Ephesians 4:21 (ESV)

The Father of Lies

Remember the spiritual battle rages all around us, even though we cannot see it with our own eyes. Until Jesus returns again in final victory, Satan will continue inflicting as much pain as he can, claiming as many victims as possible. As Christians, we can expect to face attacks from the enemy as he works relentlessly to discourage, dissuade, and divide us.

Look at how Jesus describes Satan in John 8:44 (ESV): "There is no truth in him. When he lies, he speaks out of his own character, for he is a liar and the father of lies."

Paul understood this well, which is why the very first piece of spiritual armor we strap onto our bodies is the belt of truth. The enemy is not omnipotent, as much as he may wish that were so. He cannot control you and hear your thoughts, but he *can* influence you and whisper untruths in your ear.

Have you ever felt unworthy, completely *less than*, and wondered what in the world your purpose on this earth could possibly be? The voice whispering that you are worthless is not of God. That is the voice of the father of lies, and yes, he is constantly muttering lies into your ears. When you accepted Jesus as your Lord and Savior, he sent the Holy Spirit to dwell within you, and he speaks to you as well. You can tell these voices apart by the way they speak to you. The voice of the Holy Spirit *convicts*. The voice of the enemy *condemns*.

So you forgot about your history exam and didn't study. Your grade reflects as much, and you are terrified about what your parents will say when they find out. The voice that tells you, "I am so stupid," is the voice of the enemy. The voice that says, "I made a mistake, and I am still worthy," is the voice of the Holy Spirit.

Let's say you spent the night with some friends, and after their parents went to bed, you and your friends collectively decided to watch a movie you knew was inappropriate. The voice that whispered, "Who cares? My mom will never know, and all my friends will think I'm lame if I say *no*," is the voice of the enemy. The voice that says, "This is wrong; I am strong enough to say *no*, even if everyone else says *yes*," is the voice of the Holy Spirit.

Your friend said something that really hurt you deeply. You haven't spoken in a few days, and if you are being honest, you are not sure you want to remain friends. The voice that tells you, "I can't forgive them because they cannot be trusted; they will only hurt me again," is the voice of the enemy. The voice that says, "They hurt me, but I can show forgiveness even if our friendship is no longer the same," is the voice of the Holy Spirit.

Learn to pause and listen for the difference between the voice of the father of lies and the voice of the Holy Spirit. By strapping on the belt of truth, you will be able to discern between the enemy's deception and God's truth.

Truth versus Deception

Philosophically, this question of "What is truth?" could lead to numerous tangents and discussions—all of which would likely make our heads spin.

In our world today, relativism rules. By accepting this ideology, we are trusting our culture and society to tell us what is true and that essentially no truth is absolute. Much to Satan's delight, we are now encouraged to embrace a blasé attitude about truth, often proclaiming to one another, "You do you!" We are taught that absolute truths are narrow-minded and that standing for said truths openly can result in a dislike, an unfollow, or (even worse) public shaming.

Yet, as Christians, our truth is not based on the ever-changing, always-moving cultural norms and what society deems is right and appropriate. Our truth comes from God and the revelations he shares with us through his infallible Word. What does this mean exactly? It means that truth is not defined by our own subjective standards; it is determined by the Source of truth himself. God's truth is our foundation, and it is rock solid.

If we flip in our Bibles to the book of John, we find where Pilate, the Roman governor in charge of Jesus's trial, also questioned, "What is truth?"

> Pilate: So You are a king?
>
> Jesus: You say that I am king. For this I have been born, and for this I have come into the cosmos: to demonstrate the power of truth. Everyone who seeks truth hears My voice.
>
> Pilate (to Jesus): What is truth?
>
> Pilate left Jesus to go and speak to the Jewish people.
>
> Pilate (to the Jews): I have not found any cause for charges to be brought against this man. (John 18:37–38 *The Voice*)

After his brief exchange with Jesus, Pilate pronounced Jesus innocent to the mob that had formed. Yet Jesus was still flogged and handed over for crucifixion. It appears that Pilate also felt that the truth was relative. Pilate's truth was that Jesus was innocent, but the Jews' truth proclaimed Jesus as guilty. For the sake of fairness, Pilate washed his hands of the entire matter and let the Jews follow their truth. In essence, Pilate gave Jesus to the Jews and said, "You do you."

Pilate did not realize when he asked the question, "What is truth?" that he was looking at the answer. *Jesus* is the truth. Jesus does not simply tell the truth; he defines what truth is. Jesus is the personification of truth. When we say that *truth* can change our lives, we are saying that *Jesus* can change our lives.

So if Jesus is the truth, what is deception? That's right—the father of lies, the deceiver of the world. Take just a few minutes to look up the following verses and write them in the following spaces:

John 14:6

Revelation 12:9

What do these two passages explain about the nature of Jesus and the nature of Satan?

The Belt of Truth—Then versus Now

When preparing for battle, the belt (or *balteus* as it was called in Latin) was the first piece of protective equipment a Roman soldier would have strapped onto his body. It was made of leather with an apron of straps that hung in the front to cover the soldier's lower abdomen and groin, providing protection and a place to hang his sword. The leather apron straps were covered with small brass plates to offer maximum coverage. The belt was strapped closely to the soldier's body and used to tuck up his tunic so he would not get tripped up in battle. This was for practicality. Men and women in ancient times typically wore long tunics, which would have understandably gotten in the way whenever a soldier needed to run or fight. Thus they "girded their loins" by tucking their long tunics into their leather belts. A Roman soldier could not be battle-ready without first donning his belt, which in essence held his armor together.

Similarly, Paul gives Christians a call to action in Ephesians 6:14 when he tells us to stand firm with the belt of truth buckled around our waist. With the belt of truth strapped securely around us, we are prepared to battle Satan's lies with God's truth. In essence, the truth holds everything together (Col. 1:17).

Satan's Propaganda

We all live in the danger zone, vulnerable to an attack of darts poisoned with the enemy's lies. How susceptible are you to Satan's propaganda? Take a minute and identify God's truth versus the lies of the enemy. Mark an "X" over Satan's propaganda and highlight God's truth with a colored pencil or pen.

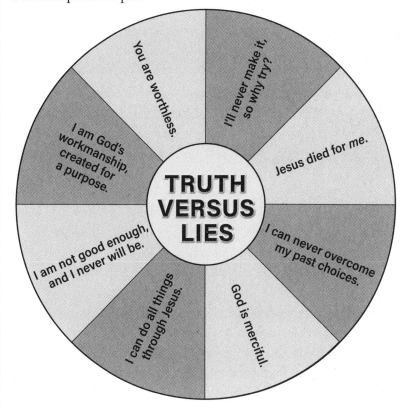

Freedom from the Enemy's Snare

The Bible helps us separate the truth from Satan's lies. When we accept what God says about Jesus (he is the only way to God) and about us (we are loved, forgiven, and worthy), then we are able to walk in the freedom of God's truth instead of the shadow of doubt or shame cast by the enemy.

Satan does not sleep and works tirelessly to ensnare us in his web of deception. However, instead of creepy spider webs, imagine enticing cotton candy. It's just as sticky. The devil's lies are usually cleverly masked in an appealing package. He counts on our naïveté and inability to see through his deceptions, and before we know it, we can become trapped.

John 8:32 says, "And you will know the truth, and the truth will set you free." Our truth in Jesus and God's Word is personal, timeless, and always relevant. This truth is a one-size-fits-all belt that we can strap around our waists and always depend on to guide us as we defend against the enemy's lies.

An Activity for Parents and Tweens:
Armor Design—The Belt of Truth

 This week, work on constructing your own belts of truth. Remember we are working on building our personalized armor to prepare for the messy, entertaining battle coming at the end of this study!

Use materials you have lying around the house for an extra challenge. This is an activity that fits within any budget, so be creative and have fun!

While you work on your belt designs this week, talk about some of the lies you hear in your head. What does the father of lies whisper in your ear? What about the voice of the Holy Spirit? Is his voice present as well? Hold hands and rebuke the enemy with John 8:32: "You will know the truth, and the truth will set you free" (CSB). Remind the enemy *aloud* that you belong to the body of Christ and that Satan has no place in your head or your home. Thank God for his goodness and ask for discernment to mute the voice of the father of lies and magnify the voice of the Holy Spirit in all your choices—great and small. Consider using the following prayer if you are uncomfortable saying your own:

Heavenly Father,

I sometimes get tripped up by the voices in my head, and I have trouble knowing which is your truth and which is a lie that Satan whispers in my ear. Please give me discernment to tell the difference. Quiet the enemy's lies and deception so that still, quiet voice of the Holy Spirit is the only voice I hear.

As for you, Satan, I claim John 8:32, and my Father tells me that I will know the truth and the truth will set me free. I do not belong to you. You do not control me. I belong to the body of Jesus Christ, and he is the ruler of my heart. I command you to leave in Jesus's name. Do not return!

Father, please send your Holy Spirit to guide me, to instruct me, to gently rebuke me, and most importantly, to draw me closer to you. Thank you for the provision you've given against the enemy's lies. Help me to remember to strap on my belt of truth and stand firm on the foundation of your Word. I love you, God.

It's in your Son's precious name I pray,
Amen.

Calling Workshop Apprentices!
Project: Belt of Truth

Materials needed:

- Cardboard (can use old mailing boxes), poster board, or that empty cereal box you finished off for breakfast this morning
- Masking or duct tape
- Scissors or box cutter
- Markers
- Yardstick or ruler

- Sharpie pen or paint
- A belt already hanging in your closet or tucked in your dresser
- Measuring tape
- Optional: Shoestrings or kite string

Step 1: Using the template in the Appendix, draw six straps for each soldier with a Sharpie pen on your cardboard. Each belt will need six straps, so think about how much cardboard or poster board your family may need ahead of time. For example, if you are making three belts, you will need 18 straps. Use a yardstick or ruler to keep your lines straight. The straps should be long enough to create a loop (for sliding over the belt), so keep that in mind as you are measuring for length.

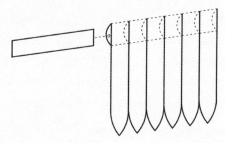

Step 2: Once the straps are drawn, use a box cutter or scissors to cut the straps out. *Parents: Box cutters should be used by adults or with adult supervision.*

Step 3: Adorn your straps with Sharpie ink or paint. You may choose to add one or more of the following Bible verses on *truth*:

- John 6:47
- Psalm 43:3
- 1 John 3:18
- Ephesians 6:14
- John 8:32
- Psalm 145:18

Step 4: Fold the top of each strap over so that it creates a loop. Use the masking or duct tape to secure the loop in place. Repeat this for the rest of the straps.

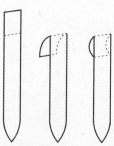

Step 5: Take a belt you already own and slide each strap onto the belt so they hang like this:

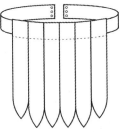

Note: If you do not have a belt on hand, use the tape measure to measure each person's waist.

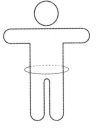

The yardstick will help you keep a steady hand as you draw the length you need on your cardboard (old Amazon boxes work great for this). Each belt needs to be three to four inches wide. Length with vary. Poke three holes in each end of the belt with your scissors or box cutter. Then run shoestrings or kite string through each hole on both sides of the belt, which you will use to tie the two sides together.

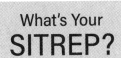

What's Your
SITREP?

It's time for a situation report, so let's check your understanding and dig deeper into the context of Chapter Two.

1. How do you know and decide when something is true?

2. Is there such a thing as absolute truth—something that is true at all times in all places? Talk with Mom or Dad about why you think so or not.

3. Look up John 17:15–17 and write it in the space below. What does Jesus pray? What does it mean to be set apart by the truth?

4. Check a different translation for John 17:15–17 than you used in the previous question, and write the new translation in the space below. Is it different, and if it is, how so? Which translation makes more sense to you?

5. Look up the following verses and write them in the spaces below:

   a. Psalm 145:18

   b. Philippians 4:8

   c. What can we conclude about truth from these two passages?

6. How can you let the truth that is Jesus change your life? Take a minute with your mom or dad to pray about this right now.

7. Read James 1:22–25 and 1 Timothy 4:7–8. Discuss with your parent(s) what these verses say you can do to help bulk up your spiritual muscles.

THIS WEEK'S **BATTLE PLAN**

1. Choose a Bible verse we have read within this study so far and personalize it in the space below. For example, for John 8:32, you might write, "And I will know the truth, and the truth will set me free." *Battle tactic: Personalizing Scripture reinforces the relevancy of God's Word for each of us.*

2. Continue to pray the armor of God over yourself and your family each day this week.

Letters from the Battlefield

Dear Friend,

For a little while now, I've had moments where I've doubted my own self-worth. Whether it was feeling like anyone didn't really care if I showed up, or if I just barely missed a goal I set for myself, I ended up feeling unworthy and unsure. I found myself wondering what my purpose in life might be. And it didn't help that I often felt like I couldn't open up to anyone about this because I worried they would judge me or think I'm weak.

Not too long ago, I had a few of the worst weeks in my life, where I felt lonely and full of self-doubt every minute of every day. I had gone on a trip with my family, then immediately became very sick and missed a lot of school right after getting home. High school is already tough. Missing three weeks of schoolwork doesn't make it any easier. The holiday break started as I was just beginning to feel better. Suddenly, I was busy with family celebrations and travel. I didn't have any time to catch up on my work.

Before I knew it, school was less than a week away from starting back up and I had almost a month of homework that needed to be done in less than a week's time. It didn't help that the most difficult practices of the year for my swim team were that same week as well. I felt overwhelmed and hopeless because I didn't think I could do all of the work. I was hearing thoughts in my head: _Am I good enough? Was this worth it? I_

can't do this. There is no way out. Thankfully, I realized the enemy was at work with his lies and I could have
chosen to continue to listen, had it not been for two
key moments.

During the first week, I felt absolutely terrible. I
couldn't stop thinking about how much work I had to do,
and every time I looked at my list, it made the situation
even worse. My first year in high school had been difficult
but had never been this overwhelming or stressful. One
night while I was getting ready for bed, I was standing in
my bathroom, sobbing to myself, thinking that I wasn't
strong enough to deal with the pressure. I cried out to
God, asking him to say something, anything, that would
make it better. It seemed like an eternity, but just a few
seconds later, I heard these words spoken in my mind:
"Be still and know that I am God."

I opened my Bible and read through Psalm 46. I felt a
calmness that I had never felt before. Everything melted
away except for those eight words—words that spoke
God's truth. After that night, I still struggled a bit with
all I had left to do, but it seemed easier and I felt positive and hopeful. I thought the worst was over. But
sadly, the enemy is clever and has ways of using your
doubts if you let your guard down to try to discourage
you and pull you away from God.

Not long after that, I was finally finished with all of
my work and feeling confident. When I made it back to
my team's swim practice, all of those feelings of hope
and joy just melted away. Our practices that week were
test sets, with really difficult timed swimming exercises
without much rest between. I failed to do my set in time,

even though I had met these goals many times before. Despite the fact that I hadn't been able to attend practice in weeks, I was embarrassed and all of the positive and hopeful feelings disappeared. Using my own feelings of doubt, the enemy was once again at work with lies and deception.

When I got home, I told my parents I felt like a failure and unworthy of their love. They sat down and talked to me, trying to comfort me, but to no avail. Nothing seemed to be working until my parents began to pray for me. Sitting on either side of me, while they were praying, I could feel the Holy Spirit inside of me, telling me to keep going and how loved and worthy I am. For the first time in what felt like forever, I believed in myself again. Not only that, but I believed in God's truth even more than before, which I didn't know was possible.

I know that I will still set expectations for myself that sometimes are unattainable and will be disappointed in myself if I fail to reach them. But because I know God's truth—that he loves me so much that he sent his Son to die for me—I can embrace his truth and start feeling confident about myself as God arms me for battle, even when I might feel sad or disappointed. He's given this truth to all of us in the Bible, which is why reading his Word and talking to him is the most important thing we can do.

The enemy fears those who he knows are instrumental in God's plan and will stop at nothing to try and tear that person away from God. He will try to make you feel hopeless and unworthy, just like he did to me. However, if you choose to embrace God and put on your belt of truth for protection, the enemy cannot overtake you. Every time you feel the negative thoughts creeping closer, whispering that you aren't good enough, know that just means the enemy is scared of you and your relationship with the Lord. God loves you beyond human reason, and the last thing he wants you to do is doubt his truth and love. Because, to God, you are priceless.

Sincerely,
Jacob

~

Dear Friend,

The enemy has a way of making you feel isolated and alone. When you allow sin to come into your heart, life can become dark and confusing. For years, I have allowed anxiety to rule in my life. I remember from a very young age being so anxious that I couldn't sleep. I was anxious that my heart would stop beating. I would get sharp pains in my chest, and I would have trouble breathing because I would be consumed with this fear. I was probably around the age of six at the time.

My parents began to lay hands on me and pray, we cried out to God that he would deliver me from anxiety. We prayed for the peace of God, and he answered our prayers. I did not struggle with anxiety for the next ten years. While I would still have moments where I was anxious, the panic attacks stopped.

However, in my sophomore year, I switched to a new school and my anxiety returned. I began to really struggle with identity; my new school was really hard academically, so it was a struggle to adjust. Additionally, I had to make all new friends. I was anxious about grades, balancing my time, and so many other things. Sometimes I would be anxious for no reason at all. I wouldn't have a test or anything to worry about that day, but I couldn't help what I was feeling. I began to feel very isolated and helpless.

This is exactly what the enemy wants—for us to feel that we are alone and that there is no way out. But God, in his mercy and his overwhelming love for us, never fails to take what Satan intends for evil and turn it into something good. In the moments when I felt very anxious, my mind would be flooded with lies.

I would tell myself, "You will never be enough. You are a disappointment. You are alone in this." But God would really draw near to me in these moments. I would eventually hit a point where I would be in tears, just asking God to take away my anxiety and restore peace in my heart.

I remember one moment vividly. That day, I had failed a test that I studied really hard for and then I got in a bad fight with my parents. I was emotionally exhausted, incredibly anxious, and overwhelmed with all of the expectations that I had put on myself. I went into my room, fell on my knees, and told God everything. I told him how I felt I would never be a good enough daughter, student, Christian, or friend. God responded to me by putting Romans 5:1-2 on my heart: "Therefore, since we have been justified through faith, we have peace with God through our Lord Jesus Christ, through whom we have gained access by faith into this grace in which we now stand. And we boast in the hope of the glory of God" (NIV).

I felt him tell me that I don't have to be "enough" because of Jesus. He is enough. From that moment on, I began to understand grace. God has taught me a great deal through my journey with anxiety. I've learned that Satan tends to target people that God has big plans for. If you have the potential to be powerful in the kingdom of God, Satan will do everything he can to separate you from him.

I allowed anxiety to take root in my heart by trying to take control and by allowing myself to believe lies. I began to realize the importance of guarding my heart and surrounding myself with the truth. I started to intentionally avoid comparing myself to other girls on Instagram, believing that I wasn't pretty enough, and avoid comparing my grades to others, believing that I wasn't smart enough.

What lies have you allowed to creep into your life? Step back and take every thought captive. Know that anxiety is one of Satan's biggest tools in order to drive a gap between you and God. Whenever you begin to believe lies, remind yourself that you are a child of God. Combat the lies of Satan with the truth of God's Word.

Be encouraged,
Madi

Chapter Three

THE BREASTPLATE OF RIGHTEOUSNESS

This Good News tells us how God makes us right in his sight.
This is accomplished from start to finish by faith. As the Scriptures say,
"It is through faith that a righteous person has life."

Romans 1:17 (NLT)

A Choice for Right Living

Following the belt of truth, Paul instructs us to put on the breastplate of righteousness (Eph. 6:14), which helps us make *right* choices as Christians. The next piece of spiritual armor comes after the belt of truth, because in order to know what is *right*, we must know what is *true*. Just like the truth, righteousness comes from God, not from ourselves.

How does the enemy keep us from living a righteous life? His battle strategy is simple: he tempts us into sin. Okay, so what is sin? Sin is any word, thought, or action that falls short of God's will. Take a minute to look up the following verses and write them in the following spaces:

James 1:14–15

Romans 7:24–25

We have already established there is an enemy, Satan, whose sole purpose is to separate us from God by tempting us into sin. In Genesis 3, we remember the serpent tempted Eve into partaking of the forbidden fruit, which she also shared with Adam. This became known as *original sin* or *the fall.* We also know Adam and Eve were ashamed and felt guilty for their actions because Scripture reveals they hid from God. Of course, God was upset, and as a result of their sin, Adam and Eve faced the consequences of their choice and were forced to leave the garden forever.

After the first sin in the Garden of Eden, our relationship with God was broken. The Old Testament is filled with examples of godly men and women who chose to seek God, but there was no perfect human—at least there wasn't until God sent Jesus to save us. Remember this is why the story of Jesus is called the good news!

> For the wages of sin is death, but the free gift of God is eternal life in Christ Jesus our Lord. (Rom. 6:23 ESV)

We are all sinners. Whether or not we are conscious of all our choices that dishonor God, each of us is guilty of committing sins *daily*. Romans 3:23 says, "For all have sinned and fall short of the glory of God" (NIV).

Let's pause and think about this for a minute. What does it mean to fall short of the glory of God? *Falling short* means we fail to meet the standard or expectation for which we hoped. In other words, we miss the target. Imagine shooting an arrow at a target and the arrow whistles right by without ever coming close to hitting its intended goal. We cannot ever meet the mark when it comes to attaining God's glory. Why? Because we are not Jesus. We are imperfect people living in a broken world. There is no amount of good works or effort on our part that could ever help us attain the glory of God.

We are taught from a young age that good behavior is rewarded. My own children went through no small number of stickers and prizes during potty training. We reward athletes with accolades and scholarship dollars, which could eventually lead to endorsement opportunities. Work is typically incentive-based. Most people are paid for their time and effort, whether completing chores or completing a marketing plan. Think of all the rewards-based systems in place throughout our society. Take a few minutes and talk with your mom or dad about what those might be and write them in the following spaces:

1.

2.

3.

4.

5.

God gives us the reward up front, and he offers it to us freely and solely by his grace alone. It is up to us to choose whether or not we accept his gift. Nothing we could ever do would make us worthy of such a precious gift. No number of stickers or in-depth training or personal triumphs could help us hit the mark of attaining God's glory. This is why we need Jesus and why God's unfathomable sacrificial love is such a priceless gift. Again, we are sinners. Anything less than the perfection of Jesus Christ falls short of the glory of God. This isn't to shame you or me. It's simple truth. Just like experiencing spiritual warfare, committing sin is not a matter of *if*; it is a matter of *when*. However, hopefully you are realizing the plan of redemption is not just good news—it's amazing news!

Jesus, who had never experienced sin, took ours from us—those who were born into sin and could not know righteousness on our own (2 Cor. 5:21). He did this so we could become righteous through him in the sight of God. Talk about a game changer!

Which Is Worse?

Are some sins worse than others? Rate the following sins, from the most offensive to the least offensive, with 1 being the most offensive and 9 being the least.

___ You lied to your teacher and said your homework was complete, but you simply left it at home. You ask if you can email it to her after school, and then you spend lunch rushing to complete the assignment. Whew! She didn't even take any points off.

___ You kissed that special someone, and it was so awesome. You were careful not to take it further physically, but you can just imagine how wonderful it would be.

___ You find ten dollars on the floor in the school bathroom, and no one else is with you. You have no idea who dropped it and decide to keep the money. Later, you overhear a classmate muttering about missing money from their backpack. You wonder if the missing money is the ten dollars you found, but you remain silent. After all, it may not really be theirs.

___ You yelled at your mom because she can be so annoying! How many times have you answered the same question over and over and over? Geez, maybe now she'll remember, even though you can tell her feelings were hurt when you raised your voice. You feel a little bad, but hopefully she won't ask the same question again.

Black versus White versus Gray Areas

Some sins are more obvious. For example, the Ten Commandments (Exod. 20:1–17) are perfectly clear about some areas of sin that are defined in the Bible as black and white:

1. Do not have any other gods before our one true God.
2. Do not make idols and worship them.
3. Do not take the Lord's name in vain.

___ You were offered a drink at a friend's party. Everyone at the party was underage, and you knew it was wrong. However, you feel proud that you only took a sip but declined a whole cup. It was a win-win. Your friends don't think you're lame, and your parents will never know.

___ You borrowed a jacket from your friend, and it looks so good on you! You always hear compliments when you wear it. Your friend has asked for it back, but you consider telling them you lost it. After all, if you don't wear it around them, they will never know the truth.

___ One of your friends always has the latest and greatest gadget. I mean, how do their parents afford all that stuff? You think about it a lot and pretty consistently ask your parents what it will take for you to get one of the new phones that literally everyone but you seems to have. That would be the coolest!

___ You would never act on it, but you really like how you feel when you look at certain pictures. It was an accident, but a photo popped up on your computer while you were working on a project for school. Now you think about those kinds of pictures a lot.

___ Your friend is cool enough, but he can be super annoying. You and your other friends discuss at length how annoying that one friend can be when he's not around, but you never say anything to his face. That would hurt him.

4. Remember the Sabbath and keep it holy.
5. Honor your father and mother.
6. Do not murder.
7. Do not commit adultery.
8. Do not steal.
9. Do not give false testimony (lie) against your neighbor.
10. Do not covet (be jealous of) your neighbor.

But what about the gray areas? Drinking, dating, kissing, vaping, smoking, clothing, music, movies, television, spending your money—while some areas may be more obvious than others, some of these things are not inherently wrong. How do you know what the *right* choice is? Remember, a *sin* is any word, thought, or action that falls short of God's glory and will for us. When you accepted Jesus, your sins were forgiven and he sent the Holy Spirit to dwell within you. It bears repeating: the Holy Spirit speaks to you, but so does the enemy. Even though the enemy cannot hear your thoughts, he has studied your behavior patterns and knows how to tempt you into sinning. And guess what? We all make mistakes and sometimes make a choice that falls short of God's will for us.

For this reason, as Christians, we should confess our sins, both known and unknown, to God regularly. Jesus has already paid the price for our sins, but it is not a universal *get-out-of-jail-free* card that we can use whenever we feel the whim. We should still try to make the *right* choice to honor God.

Sin Is Sin. Period.

Sin is sin, friends. All sins are equal in the sense that every sin separates us from God. This is why we should strive to pause and listen for the voice of the Holy Spirit to guide us before making a choice, however insignificant it may seem. The enemy is smart, enticing, and he is always looking for clever new ways to trip you up so that you make a choice that does not honor God or the person he is calling you to be. We need Jesus, because we cannot live a righteous life without him.

The Breastplate of Righteousness—Then versus Now

Ephesians 6:14 says, "Stand therefore, having fastened on the belt of truth, and having put on the breastplate of righteousness" (ESV). Why do you think Paul used a breastplate to describe righteousness?

The Roman soldier's breastplate was covered in metal plates and fastened around both the soldier's chest and back, and then it was held in place by his belt. Front-only coverage would assume a soldier was never attacked from behind, which we know is not true. A cunning and ruthless enemy would certainly attack an exposed back. The breastplate protected a soldier's vital organs, preventing an enemy's arrow from piercing his heart or lungs. The armor was handmade for each soldier, so it fit him perfectly. While it couldn't prevent all the enemy's blows, it proved very effective when the soldier was engaged in hand-to-hand combat.

In Isaiah 59:17, the passage paints a picture of the Messiah, who we know to be Jesus Christ, putting on "righteousness as a breastplate" in his battle against injustice, unrighteousness, and corruption in the world. In the New Testament, we learn how God, through his Son, lends his own righteousness to those who believe in him. However, we also learn that righteousness is not something we could ever earn on our own or through good deeds. This is a tough concept, and modern-day Christians are not the only ones who question how to live a righteous life.

When the Galatians asked Paul how they should try to finish the work begun by the Holy Spirit, Paul reminded them they received the Holy Spirit because they believed the message about Jesus, not because they obeyed the law of Moses (Gal. 3:2–3). He asked them, "After starting your new lives in the Spirit, why are you now trying to become perfect by your own human effort?" (Gal. 3:3 NLT).

Righteousness Is a Gift We Receive through Our Faith in Jesus

> *When it counts*, I want to be found belonging to Him, not clinging to my own righteousness based on law, but actively relying on the faithfulness of the Anointed One. *This is true* righteousness, supplied by God, acquired by faith. (Phil. 3:9 *The Voice*)

The only way to become righteous, or justified, before God is to accept that Jesus died on the cross and paid the blood price for our sins (2 Cor. 5:21). It is *this* righteousness that protects our hearts from the enemy's arrows—defending against his attacks from both the front and back. Our best defensive weapon against spiritual darkness is the righteousness that comes from faith through Jesus. When we live the way God calls us to live as Christians, we can stand against spiritual attacks that would seek to destroy vital areas of our lives.

Be Aware, Not Afraid

The enemy works hard to oppose the power of God and to destroy the work of God. Our protection against these attacks comes in the form of spiritual armor that covers truth, righteousness, faith, peace—all aspects of God's character that grow within us as we develop our relationship with Jesus. God's armor protects us, and it does so quite effectively. We are to keep our focus on the ways of the Word, despite Satan's efforts to shift our focus to the ways of the world.

The Holy Spirit is our Helper, sent by Jesus to guide and empower us. We should be aware of our enemy but not afraid of him. Save your energy as you strive to make the right choices and live a righteous life.

Paul also wrote about this in his letter to Titus. He explained that God's grace is our motivation for righteous or right living. In this letter, Paul said right living is essential for Christians because Jesus "gave His body for our sakes and will not only break us free from the chains of wickedness, but He will also prepare a community uncorrupted by the world that He would call His own—people who are passionate about doing the right thing" (Titus 2:14, *The Voice*).

Our belief in God is reflected in every decision we make. Process that for a second. When we accept Jesus, we receive salvation. We don't grow in our salvation, however, but we do actively grow in our faith. After we accept Jesus into our hearts, we spend the rest of our lives in the process of sanctification. That's a fancy way of saying that once we come to know Jesus, we want to make better choices, but we are already saved by our faith and belief in God.

> This Good News tells us how God makes us right in his sight. This is accomplished from start to finish by faith. As the Scriptures say, "It is through faith that a righteous person has life." (Rom. 1:17 NLT)

Living a righteous life does not mean living a perfect life, so don't put that kind of pressure on yourself. We all mistakes, and we make them often. Again, it is through Jesus's sacrifice and God's grace that we can strap on the breastplate of righteousness.

An Activity for Parents and Tweens:
Armor Design—The Breastplate of Righteousness

 This week, work on constructing your own breastplate of righteousness. Remember we are working on building our own personalized armor to prepare for the messy, entertaining battle coming at the end of this study!

Use materials you have lying around the house for an extra challenge. This is an activity that fits within any budget, so be creative and have fun!

This week, as you work on your breastplate designs, take some time to talk about the tough choices you're faced with today. What does *right* living as a modern Christian look like? Discuss some of those gray areas of life choices and how you decide which is the right choice when faced with those circumstances.

Hold hands and pray together as a family this week, asking God to give you the courage and discernment to make right choices, no matter how inconsequential the decision might seem. Rebuke the enemy whenever you feel him tempting you to sin, and remember to speak aloud! Otherwise, he cannot hear you. Thank God for his divine wisdom to craft spiritual armor that can help us from falling into Satan's snares of sin, giving us the freedom to stand firm on God's truth and the knowledge that we are making choices which honor God's will for our lives.

If you are uncomfortable praying on your own, consider reading the following prayer aloud together.

Most Merciful Father,

In your infinite wisdom, you crafted the most perfect defense for me against an enemy who relentlessly pursues. Thank you for loving me so much that you crafted a breastplate that fits me perfectly. The enemy has studied me and knows my weakness, but he does not know the number of hairs on my head like you do. He did not craft me with love and purpose in my mother's tummy like you did. Thank you for loving me beyond what I could ever comprehend. Of course, a loving Father would provide for his child, and I wear the spiritual armor you've given me with humility and honor.

Give me the strength to refuse the enemy's enticing temptations, God. Help me to make the right choice always—the choice that honors you and the person you have called me to be. When I fail, Father (and I know I make mistakes), please forgive me and lead me to those right choices once again.

Satan, I rebuke you in Jesus's name. You are relentless, but my God pursues me more than you. He lifts me up when I fall. Even though you try to separate me from my Heavenly Father through acts of sin, you are powerless next to God. I command you to leave in Jesus's name; do not return.

I love you, Father. Thank you for loving me so much that you sent your one and only Son to die for my sins. Thank you for the gift of salvation and that I am made righteous through my faith in him.

In Jesus's holy name I pray,
Amen

What's Your
SITREP?

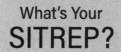

It's time for a situation report, so let's check your understanding and dig deeper into the context of Chapter Three.

1. What is sin?

2. Read Romans 3:23 and write it in the space below. What does this passage say about all people?

3. Talk about a situation or an area of your life where you struggle to do the right thing.

4. Is there something you should confess to God right now? Write it in the space below and talk about it with your mom or dad.

5. Where does righteousness come from?

6. Look up the following Scriptures and write them in the following spaces:

   a. Proverbs 21:21

   b. 1 Timothy 6:11

   c. Proverbs 4:23

    d. Matthew 6:33

    e. Philippians 4:8

7. What do the verses above inspire Christians to do?

8. Read Titus 3:2–8. What is Paul's call to action?

9. Read 2 Corinthians 5:21. Rewrite it in your own words below and talk with your parent(s) about what it means to you.

10. Why is it important to protect our hearts?

11. What are three ways you might seek righteous or *right* living?

THIS WEEK'S **BATTLE PLAN**

1. Clear away the clutter in your heart. Think about how clutter can overwhelm your room or home. What happens when you clear the clutter away? You can breathe easier and move about more freely. This is what confession does for us; it declutters our hearts from the *mess of sin. Battle tactic: Confessing our sins removes the foothold our enemy attempts to secure in our hearts in order to tempt us into further sin.*

   a. This week, make a conscious effort to confess your sins to God—both known and unknown. Place your hand over your heart and be aware of the vital organ God protects within you by bestowing upon you the breastplate of righteousness.

   b. Write your confessions down and talk with your parent(s) about how it feels to clear the clutter from your heart.

2. Continue to pray the armor of God over yourself and your family each day this week.

Letters from the Battlefield

Dear Friend,

Growing up, I didn't have the stereotypical picture-perfect family with two happily married parents who seemed just head over heels in love with each other as they were when they were still dating. That's not to say that's how every family is, of course! It's common knowledge that nobody is perfect, so that naturally extends to the family category (with God being the only exception). Every family has their ups and downs, victories and defeats, happiness and heartache. That's reality.

And, sadly, reality can hurt . . . horribly. I can testify.

My parents were married in December 1999, exactly five months before I would come into the picture. By the time I was two years old, they were divorced, with my mom and me living on our own. It would be a few years after that when I would hear the word <u>drugs</u> for the first time. Of course, my innocent brain did not register the word as older people would. After all, I was just a little girl. When I asked my mom about drugs, she responded carefully, "Drugs are bad medicine that people take when they shouldn't, baby. They get addicted to them, and they're really, <u>really</u> hard to stop taking."

Instead of satiating my curiosity, that response raised more questions, such as, <u>What does addicted mean?</u> <u>Why is this medicine bad if medicine is supposed to help</u> <u>people when they are sick? Above all, if it is bad for you,</u> <u>then why take it in the first place?</u> Though my questions were logical, the actions of human beings, as I would soon learn, were anything but.

I don't have a lot of early memories of my dad. When I asked my mom and grandparents (both his and my mom's) about him and where he was, I heard the same answer: he was living in Colorado. Why he was living there, I didn't know. I just shrugged, accepted the answer, and went back to playing.

Soon after, I learned about rehab—the place where people go when they are addicted to drugs and want to stop taking them. By now, I was in elementary school, which required us to take D.A.R.E. (Drug Abuse Resistance Education). Local police officers served as our teachers during the course, and needless to say, I became well versed in narcotics, alcohol, and other addictive substances. But, most importantly, during these classes, they drilled the D.A.R.E. motto into the minds of my peers and me, with three simple but powerful words: Just say no.

Throughout the next several years, my dad moved in and out of rehab, which means I rarely saw him. I spent most of that time with my mom. I was barely two months into my freshman year when my mom and her boyfriend at the time got into an argument and left the house in the middle of the night. I let my sister sleep in my room and waited for them to return. Mom reappeared briefly with a lady she had only just met, but then she disappeared again. I fell asleep sometime after three or four o'clock in the morning and soon woke up to get ready for school. My mom was not home, but my grandmother (her mom) and my mom's boyfriend were. They explained that my mom was in the hospital. My sister and I moved in with my grandparents, mom received the help she needed and returned a few months later, and things were normal again for a while. Then, during the summer before my junior year of high school, I would face the biggest obstacle life has ever thrown at me—the death of a loved one.

My dad had contracted staph and didn't go into the hospital for treatment until it was really severe. My grandfather (his dad) took him to the emergency room himself. When I heard about my dad's illness, the strangest feeling fell over me, and to this day I can't really explain it. Suddenly, one thought plagued my mind nonstop: I needed to see Dad, and it needed to be <u>soon</u>.

<u>Soon</u> turned out to be a few days later. I was passing through town and decided to visit my dad while I could. When I entered his hospital room (draped in protective clothing), I greeted him and he cheerfully responded, despite his tired, sickly appearance. Before I knew it, we had launched into a conversation about my plans for the future and what I wanted to make of myself. This, of course, revolved mainly around continuing education in college. A few minutes later, I needed to leave, but not before exchanging pleasantries: "I love you," "I hope you get better soon," and "Come see me again." We sealed it with an air hug, and that was it.

During the early hours of the morning about three weeks later, my mom, her parents, and my aunt came into my room. Mom was crying uncontrollably as she held me close. Dad was gone.

There are two sayings that I have always lived by: "God gives his hardest battles to his strongest soldiers" (Habeeb Akande), and "[God] will not let you be tempted beyond what you can bear" (1 Cor. 10:13 NIV). God is the one who truly knows each of us inside and out—from our very first thought to the exact number of hairs on our heads. I didn't truly realize the full extent of his power until a few days after Dad's funeral.

God knew what would happen during my lifetime when he created me, and although I've had more than my fair share of adversity, it was the people he planted in my life and the wisdom of his teaching that drove me to make the decisions that have brought me along thus far.

I didn't _have_ to say no to drugs.

I didn't _have_ to walk away.

I didn't _have_ to pretend to be who I wasn't for attention.

I didn't _have_ to move on.

It wasn't a matter of having to do anything based on what I thought was best or what I wanted to do. _No._ It was a matter of what God knew was best and what he wanted me to do. God has turned the worst adversities in my life into the greatest weapons I could ever wield when facing the start of a new day and a new challenge. They have molded me into who I am and who I want to be.

And, quite frankly, should I ever, by some miracle, be given the option to choose between the life I've lived or a "normal" one with two living, married parents, I'd choose the life God has given me. This is my story, and these are my experiences. God never gave up on me when I needed him most. And he never will.

Look to him to help guide you and make choices that honor him, and you'll never be led astray.

Sincerely,
Baylee

Chapter Four

THE SANDALS OF PEACE

And let the peace of Christ rule in your hearts . . .
Colossians 3:15 (ESV)

The Devil Is a Stinkin' Thief

As I sit here and pray what to write, the irony of my current situation is not lost on me. I have wanted to write about spiritual warfare for years. *Years.* I am passionate about the next generation of Jesus followers, who need to learn how to defend against a ruthless enemy in an unseen war. My husband and I have led many discussions with our daughters over the importance of preparing for battle, knowing your enemy, and strapping on their spiritual armor of God.

When my publisher gave the green light for this Bible study to move forward, I was (and continue to be) ecstatic. However, the enemy was less so. He has expressed his displeasure by unleashing a fierce attack on me and those I hold dear. You might wonder what that might look like. Well, let me tell you.

In the last two months, my husband had an unexpected job change, which means he transitioned to working in an office across town after working from home for the last fifteen years. It's a blessing, but the transition has been *rough*. My eldest was bitten in the face by a dog just days before Christmas. My youngest was really sick a few weeks later. A dear friend was in a car accident, totaling his vehicle. Thank goodness he was unharmed by the incident, but it was really scary. Fast-forward one week, my own children were in a car accident on the way to church. Thankfully, they were unharmed as well. I was home because my husband was sick after catching whatever virus my youngest daughter had. The address of the other driver in the car accident with my girls was . . . wait for it . . . Kicking Bird Drive. Our last name is Bird. Not even clever, Satan.

A few days later, my sick husband went back to work because he had just started a new job and didn't want to let any of his new coworkers down. When he came home that night, he said he felt like he needed to go to an after-hours clinic. Guess what? He had pneumonia. Right. Then, the next morning, my eldest child tested positive for the flu. Of course.

So as I was sitting back at my desk and praying over what to write to encourage parents and tweens as they work through the pages of this study, my cousin sent a text to check on me. I vented and ended my lament with, "Satan has stolen my peace!"

She simply wrote back, "Isn't it ironic ♪," which of course made me laugh. But she's right. Satan is a stinkin' thief.

The Good News

This is actually a perfect introduction to the sandals of peace, which is next up in our exploration of the spiritual armor God has given us. The purpose of these special shoes is to give us peace so we can share the good news and peace of Jesus with others. When life circumstances threaten to steal your peace and knock you to your knees, the sandals of peace enable you to stand firm on a foundation that the enemy cannot shake or break. Similar to what I shared here, maybe you are going through a really tough time right now. Parents divorcing, a bully at school, trouble with friends (which parents face, too), a global pandemic—any number of things can attempt to knock us off balance.

The truth is Satan can make our lives pretty miserable, but he can never, *ever* steal your salvation from you. Once you are marked as Christ's own, there are no takebacks. You are his, and his goodness and mercy are shared with you forever. The enemy would have us believe differently, so one way God helps us defend against Satan's schemes is by equipping our feet with the sandals of peace.

Peace!

What exactly does *peace* mean? Think about the vast and varied definitions and uses we see of the word *peace* in our culture. You may say that summer brings peace and refuge from homework. Your mom may think a hot bath and five minutes of quiet brings peace. (Parents, can I get an *amen*?) In the 1960s, the peace sign was a prominent symbol used as many Americans protested the war in Vietnam. Where do we see that symbol of peace today? It is still widely used on notebook designs, jewelry, clothing, and graffiti, and we see it in many other places, as well.

When we talk about the sandals of peace, or sandals of the gospel of peace as they are sometimes called, we are not referring to any cultural references of tranquility. When we talk about what comes with the sandals of peace, we are talking about the peace that surpasses all understanding (Phil. 4:7). Look up the following verses and write them in the following spaces:

Colossians 3:16

John 14:27

When life feels downright crummy and awful, we can receive and walk in the peace that God is always in control. The enemy is like a thief in the night and wants desperately to steal your shoes of peace! Satan does not work alone, either. Remember, he has an army of his own. For example, one of the enemy's soldiers is the spirit of worry. What does he steal? He steals our peace. This is a tried-and-true tactic Satan uses to knock us off balance, but the sandals of peace help us recognize and rebuke these types of spiritual attacks. When we are disoriented, disappointed, and distracted, this is when the enemy closes in, because he thinks we are weakened.

Think about some of the physiological and psychological effects of worrying. Our appetite may be affected when we worry. We may lose sleep (which happens to me frequently). When our spirits are not at rest, our bodies often follow suit. If this is how you feel, grab your Bible. Read the words of Philippians 4:6–7 aloud right now and anytime when you feel the spirit of worry threatening to overwhelm you:

> Don't be anxious about things; instead, pray. Pray about everything. He longs to hear your requests, so talk to God about your needs and be thankful for what has come. And know that the peace of God (a peace that is beyond any and all of our human understanding) will stand watch over your hearts and minds in Jesus, the Anointed One. (Phil. 4:6–7 *The Voice*)

When the enemy attacks, and he *will* attack, we will be prepared for battle with the sandals of peace strapped firmly on our feet. If we let the peace of Christ rule our hearts, the enemy will have no foothold for his lies and deception. Jesus gave us his very own reassurance of peace, a peace that is not of this world, but *his* peace. Our preparation for battle comes from Jesus's peace and the gospel—the good news about Jesus. Through this, not only do we find peace for ourselves, but we can tell others how they can have peace through God, too.

The Sandals of Peace—Then versus Now

Paul says in Ephesians 6:15, "For shoes, put on the peace that comes from the Good News so that you will be fully prepared" (NLT). Roman soldiers wore shoes called *caligae*, which would have served as the soldier's primary means of transportation. They were specifically designed to keep soldiers' feet healthy during the rigors of long marches and were very different from the sandals worn by civilian men and women of ancient times. The shoes were constructed from three layers of leather, about three quarters of an inch thick, which were pulled up and laced around the ankle. In addition, small spikes or iron hobnails were often driven into the soles of the shoes for firm footing on uneven terrain.

Just as the Roman soldier's sandals provided a firm foundation for him to stand in battle, the sandals of the gospel of peace provide Christians with the preparation and foundation we need to face life's spiritual battles. Jesus came to tell us the good news, the *gospel*, of a coming kingdom of God. It was a message that included a call to action—what Christians call *the Great Commission*.

> I am here speaking with all the authority of God, who has commanded Me to give you this commission: Go out and make disciples in all the nations. Ceremonially wash them through baptism in the name of the triune God: Father, Son, and Holy Spirit. Then disciple them. Form them in the practices and postures that I have taught you, and show them how to follow the commands I have laid down for you. And I will be with you, day after day, to the end of the age. (Matt. 28:18–20 *The Voice*)

In the original language, these words were spoken as a command, not a suggestion. This is why we call this the Great Commission. This call to action is for every follower of Jesus. If we are his disciples, we are commanded to go and make disciples of others, so, like the Roman soldier, we have some marching of our own to do. By strapping on the sandals of peace, we are ready to step forward.

Shadrach, Meshach, and Abednego

In Daniel 3, we learn about a Babylonian king named Nebuchadnezzar, who had a giant gold statue (ninety feet tall by ninety feet wide) made and put on display for all to see. Then he commanded everyone to worship his fancy new statue or else they would be thrown into a blazing furnace. Yikes! Three Jewish leaders, Shadrach, Meshach, and Abednego, refused to bow down and worship King Nebuchadnezzar's gold statue, and that made the king H-O-T.

The king ordered the three men to be brought before him, and he once more asked Shadrach, Meshach, and Abednego to bow down and worship the golden idol. They *again* refused. Scripture says the king flew into a rage, telling the men they would be thrown into the blazing furnace. He asked them which god could possibly be able to rescue them from his power. The men were not afraid, which they made clear by how they responded:

> If we are thrown into the blazing furnace, the God whom we serve is able to save us. He will rescue us from your power, Your Majesty. But even if he doesn't, we want to make it clear to you, Your Majesty, that we will never serve your gods or worship the gold statue you have set up. (Dan. 3:17–18 NLT)

As you can imagine, their refusal did not sit well with the already-angered monarch. He ordered the furnace to be heated seven times hotter than usual! Then he ordered some of his strongest men to bind Shadrach, Meshach, and Abednego and throw the three men into the furnace. Look what happens next:

> But suddenly, Nebuchadnezzar jumped up in amazement and exclaimed to his advisers, "Didn't we tie up three men and throw them into the furnace?"
>
> "Yes, Your Majesty, we certainly did," they replied.
>
> "Look!" Nebuchadnezzar shouted. "I see four men, unbound, walking around in the fire unharmed! And the fourth looks like a god!" (Dan. 3: 24–25 NLT)

God did not save Shadrach, Meshach, and Abednego from the blazing fire. He met them in the middle of it. How does God meet us in our own *furnaces* in the face of the enemy? This is important. He does not always change our circumstances, but he never abandons us to them. This is where we find our peace. We belong to God, the Almighty. We are marked as one of his own, and you better believe God keeps an eye on every single lamb in his flock. Remember he leaves the ninety-nine to save the one (Matt. 18:12).

When we find ourselves in a blazing-hot furnace, the only thing burning at the end of the day is the enemy's rear end that he cannot steal you away from a loving God who sacrificed his one and only Son just for you. That is how deeply you are loved, and with that love comes the peace of Jesus.

What Is Martyrdom?

The Greek word *martys* means *witness* or *testimony*, and it's where we get our English word for *martyrdom*. Stephen, the first Christian martyr (Acts 7:54–60), was one of many early Christian witnesses who gave their life for faith. Thankfully, not all Christians today are called to give our lives for faith. However, sharing the gospel is still dangerous in many parts of the world today. Take a few minutes and pray for missionaries and God's ambassadors who are serving in dangerous situations or who are currently imprisoned for preaching the good news.

Strength in Community

Romans 12:5 (ESV) says, "So we, though many, are one body in Christ, and individually members one of another." As the image bearers of the triune God (the Father, the Son, and the Holy Spirit), we are crafted for community and not meant to stand on our own. This is another reason Paul's analogy of the Roman soldier was so smart. Roman soldiers stood shoulder to shoulder in battle, reflecting something called the "tortoise formation." Much like the shell of a tortoise, this Roman military formation allowed soldiers to stand together, nearly impenetrable and undefeatable. Imagine if these soldiers had worn slippery shoes! Standing their ground, even in such a formidable formation, would have proven most difficult.

Paul also expounds on the topic of peace within the context of our community in his letter to Ephesus. He said, "Always be humble and gentle. Be patient with each other, making allowance for each other's faults because of your love. Make every effort to keep yourselves united in the Spirit, binding yourselves together with peace" (Eph. 4:2–3 NLT). What Paul emphasizes here is the importance of sharing a humble and forgiving attitude towards each other, which helps us keep the unity within our community that God has gifted through the Holy Spirit. Have you ever had a disagreement with a friend? Sure! We all have. Part of being in the body of Christ means forgiving one another when we make mistakes, instead of holding grudges. Much like sin separates us from God, disagreements and misunderstandings can separate us from one another within our body of Christian believers. Remember, we are stronger together.

Galatians 6:2 also instructs, "Bear one another's burdens, and so fulfill the law of Christ" (ESV). We are to help one another, encourage one another, and bind ourselves together with the peace that comes from knowing Jesus Christ. Community is a gift from God to you, and Scripture is rich with instruction about how we are to love one another. Look up the following verses and write them in the following spaces:

John 13:34–35

Ephesians 4:32

1 Peter 4:7–11

At the very center of your community is the God who created it. Our God, the Creator of all things (Col. 1:16), in his perfect wisdom, crafted us to crave what we need most aside from him—and that is one another. Satan would have us believe we are alone, and he works hard to separate each of us from our communities so that we feel desolate and afraid. Remember the truth of who you are and whose you are, holding fast to the gift of salvation through Christ and standing firm in your sandals of peace.

An Activity for Parents and Tweens:
Armor Design—The Sandals of Peace

 This week, work on constructing your own sandals of peace. Remember we are working on building our own personal armor to prepare for the messy, entertaining battle coming at the end of this study!

Use materials you have lying around the house for an extra challenge. This is an activity that fits within any budget, so be creative and have fun!

As you construct your sandals of peace, talk with one another about ways the enemy works to steal your peace. His attacks are often clever and calculated. How do you respond when you feel disoriented and separated from your community? Remember, this is a lie! You are never alone. Talk about how you personally can better defend against these types of spiritual attacks with the sandals of peace strapped firmly on your feet.

Pray together aloud as you thank God for the provision of such special shoes. Ask for determination and awareness of the enemy when he sneaks in like a thief in the night and attempts to steal your peace. Rebuke the enemy and remind him that he does not have the power to steal your peace.

If you are uncomfortable saying your own prayer, try the prewritten offering below instead.

Loving God,

You are such a good, good Father. Thank you for outfitting me with these special shoes that help me stand firm when Satan and his army attack. Thank you for the peace of Jesus, which I hold deep in my spirit. I am so thankful you love me so much that you have crafted special armor that fits me so perfectly. Help me to remember to put it on each day in preparation for the kingdom work you have called me to do.

Thank you also for the community you have gifted me and the physical reminder that I am not a lone soldier on the battlefield. We are stronger together, and I am so thankful to be a part of the body of Christ.

Satan, you cannot steal my peace. You are not that powerful, and my peace comes from Jesus, who has already conquered you. I command you to go in Jesus's name and do not return. My peace rests in the hope of the gospel, which I am called to share with others. My commission comes from God, and you cannot take that away. I command you to go to the cross, where Jesus will deal with you himself.

Forgive me when I fail you, Father God, and forgive me for my sins—both known and unknown. Help me seek you first in all things.

In Jesus's precious name I pray,
Amen.

What's Your
SITREP?

It's time for a situation report, so let's check your understanding and dig deeper into the context of Chapter Four.

1. How might we seek peace in our lives apart from Jesus? Talk with your mom or dad about how the peace of the world is different than the peace of God.

2. List the ways in which the enemy may try to steal your peace and then discuss them. Are you struggling against the enemy now?

3. Read Mark 4:35–41. Now look again at the story of Shadrach, Meshach, and Abednego in Daniel 3:13–27. In the space below, compare how the men in each passage handled their fear and worry.

4. Look up the lyrics of John Waller's "Our God Reigns Here." What is this song encouraging us to do?

5. What does Isaiah 26:3 say about how to strap on the sandals of peace?

6. Read 1 Thessalonians 5:13, Romans 1:12, and James 5:6. What do these passages say about Christian fellowship and community?

7. How might your choice to strap on the sandals of peace help another believer?

8. Look up Romans 10:15 and write it in the space below. Talk with your parent(s) about what this passage of Scripture means to you.

9. Ask the Lord to place the name of someone on your heart who needs encouragement and with whom God wants you to share about Jesus. Talk with your parent(s) about how you might share the good news with them.

.... THIS WEEK'S **BATTLE PLAN** ....

1. Ask God to place the name of someone who needs encouragement on your heart. Reach out to that person and ask if you can pray with them. Regardless of whether or not you are able to get in touch with them, pray peace over that person every day this week. Perhaps send a text or Snapchat to encourage them. *Battle tactic: We are stronger when we stand together, which also makes defending against the enemy's attacks less daunting.*

2. Continue to pray the armor of God over yourself and each member of your family. If you are having trouble remembering to pray, go back to the paper where you wrote Ephesians 6:10–19. Tape it somewhere you are sure to see it—on the bathroom mirror, on a bedside table, inside a notebook you use for school, or in another place. Set aside time to pray the armor of God aloud with your family this week.

Letters from the Battlefield

Dear Friend,

If you were to meet me for the first time, I would likely seem happy, excited, perhaps even energetic, but most certainly a little shy. However, my smile hides the anxiety that never feels far below the surface. Over the last few years, my shyness has grown and grown, becoming heavier and heavier. Only recently have I realized that I have been using my shyness as a way to protect myself from embarrassment and failure. When it doesn't work, I feel like another layer of shyness grows to buffer the fear that threatens to overwhelm me.

Despite my efforts to protect myself, there is a constant plummeting feeling in my stomach that no matter what I do, I will fail. Even when I'm doing something as simple as placing an order for food at a restaurant, that unwelcome yet familiar sinking feeling bubbles up, kind of like a volcano in my stomach. I have allowed fear to impact almost everything that I do. Slowly and slyly, fear has stolen my peace little by little. This past year, fear even robbed me of worship as I became afraid of singing publicly to God in church.

How has fear overtaken so much of my life?

When did it grow so encompassing that I feel self-conscious about ordering a meal?

Why have I allowed fear to rob me of my peace?

Fear suffocates peace. It's a silent killer, too. No one, not even those closest to me, has known the depth of my struggles with this awful feeling that never seems to go away. I've never been what my parents call an "over-sharer," and I like to think things through on the inside rather than talk about them aloud. Maybe this is why the feeling of fear has overgrown in my spirit and ruthlessly attacked the peace I know should be there.

I think Satan does this intentionally. Satan studies us and knows our weaknesses, and he works hard to break us down and make us feel terrible about ourselves. We have a choice about how we respond to him, though. We can defend against his attacks by either using the Lord and his Word or trying to battle the enemy alone. I'm here to tell you that battling alone does not work. We weren't meant to fight an army as one person, but we are equipped to battle as a community.

A few weeks ago, I attended Winter Camp with my church, and the pastor there gave a sermon on peace. I know this was not an accident. The way the pastor explained peace helped me understand and process that what I had been experiencing was a spiritual attack. Satan was trying to steal my peace! But here's what was so enlightening during this sermon, and honestly it was a game changer:

Peace is not a _what_. It's a _Who_.

Those two sentences changed my perspective of peace, and Satan's lie that I previously believed was brought into the light. He can't steal my peace, because the peace that was given to me when I accepted Jesus into my heart can never be taken away.

Philippians 4:4-7 says,

Rejoice in the Lord always; again I will say, rejoice. Let your reasonableness be known to everyone. The Lord is at hand; do not be anxious about anything, but in everything by prayer and supplication with thanksgiving let your requests be made known to God. And the peace of God, which surpasses all understanding, will guard your hearts and your minds in Christ Jesus. (ESV)

Many people have a conditional faith with God. If you do this for me, then I will do that for you. But that's not how it works. God is peace, and peace is not supposed to take away the pain. It is there to help us through the pain and persevere when the times get tough. As Dory from _Finding Nemo_ says, "Just keep swimming." Eventually, you will get through the hurt, and whatever you are going through will mold you into a person with a life-altering testimony that God can use to encourage someone else who is having trouble remembering to "just keep swimming." God is always here, waiting with his arms open wide. For you. For me. For anyone ready to accept his gift of peace.

Just keep swimming,
EK

Dear Friend,

It is very important to learn about your enemy to understand more clearly how he attacks. Learning how Satan is clever and cunning is critical to staying on the narrow path that leads to life with Jesus. Matthew 7:13-14 says, "Enter through the narrow gate. For wide is the gate and broad is the road that leads to destruction, and many enter through it. But small is the gate and narrow the road that leads to life, and only a few find it" (NIV).

From my experience, I can tell you that the devil is cunning and ruthless enough to use something positive in your life against you. Everyone on this planet is flawed in some way, and that is because of the sin that we as humans have committed. No one is perfect! Thankfully, Jesus came and paid the ultimate sacrifice so that we would not die in our sin but have eternal life. My story today is about how the enemy used someone I trusted to slowly steal and destroy my peace.

When I was in fifth grade, a friend and I started playing sports together. We spent a lot of time together, hanging out during school, at one another's houses, and before games. This continued until seventh grade, when I noticed that he was starting to make fun of me—and not like a friend poking fun of someone in a friendly way. His jests were made in a mean-hearted way. At first, I was a bit concerned over the matter, but I didn't really do anything to stop it. That was a mistake, because slowly over time, I felt sad and unenthusiastic about going to school and playing on the team.

After the season ended, the situation continued to go downhill. I started becoming angry and short-tempered with everyone around me. This happened because I was still not addressing the problem. I lost sleep at night because I felt guilty about my behavior and could not stop thinking about my friend's insults. James 1:19-20 says, "My dear brothers and sisters, take note of this: Everyone should be quick to listen, slow to speak and slow to become angry, because human anger does not produce the righteousness that God desires" (NIV).

I didn't tell anyone what was happening, and it continued for a long time. Once I even stormed out of a game because he made an unfair call, and it infuriated me. I was embarrassed about how I behaved in front of everyone at school, but my anger had boiled over since I was not dealing with it. My peace was gone. Completely gone.

I told my mom and dad about the incident but did not explain everything that had happened up to that point. I kept that in the dark, and Satan continued to use it against me. What was it doing to me personally? I could not sleep at night. I would have thoughts of him harming me throughout the day. I would just sit and think about how I should handle this problem by myself. At that time, I did not know that this was Satan trying to steal my peace, and I never thought about taking the situation before God and asking him what I should do.

Finally, I decided to tell my parents what I was going through. After talking and praying with me, they asked, "Have you asked God for advice?" I had not thought about doing that, and I immediately knew that I should stop trying to handle the situation on my own. I needed God's help. After praying and talking with my parents about it, I decided to confront my friend about how he had been treating me. He agreed to stop making fun of me. I am very glad that I asked the Lord and followed his lead in talking to my friend about his behavior and how it was affecting me. After the conversation, I felt a peace come over me that I had done the right thing.

Things did not change right away, but I had a peace about me that I did not have before because I was relying on the Lord. Today I am friends with him again, as he did change his behavior and began acting like a good friend to me. It took awhile to trust him, but over time, his actions showed me that he had truly changed.

Peace is something very valuable, and we should guard our peace from the enemy. If someone steals your peace, go to the Lord and ask for him to restore it. He is the only one who can give you the peace that passes all understanding. Sometimes the Lord prompts us to act so that our peace may be restored. In my case, I needed to talk to my friend about the issue directly, but I know that for some of you that may not be possible. Maybe you are dealing with a bully who is not your friend, or perhaps it is a family member or relative that the enemy is using to steal your peace. Satan can steal your peace using a lot of different tactics. John 10:10 says, "The thief comes only to steal and kill and destroy; I have come that they may have life, and have it to the full" (NIV).

Before he left this earth, Jesus spent time with his disciples, telling them how much God loved them and how he will care for them. In John 16:33 he said, "I have told you these things, so that in me you make have peace. In this world you will have trouble. But take heart! I have overcome the world" (NIV). Friend, when this world tries to steal your peace, remember that God is bigger than all your troubles and he has already overcome the enemy!

Sincerely,
Ethan

Chapter Five

THE SHIELD
OF FAITH

*Faith shows the reality of what we hope for; it
is the evidence of things we cannot see.*

Hebrews 11:1 (NLT)

First Line of Defense

Paul tells us in Ephesians 6:16 to "hold up the shield of faith to stop the fiery
arrows of the devil" (NLT). Even though we cannot see God, we can have
faith that he is with us. When we take up our shield of faith, we are protected from Satan's attacks not by our own strength but by putting our faith
in Jesus. Our shield of faith is our first line of defense against the enemy's
fire and spiritual darkness that we encounter as believers of Jesus Christ.

The shield of faith is different from the belt of truth, the breastplate of
righteousness, and the sandals of peace because we do not wear it. We use
it as a cover, much like a soldier would use a shield to deflect the onslaught
of enemy arrows. Raising our shield of faith means we trust and rely on
Jesus no matter what our life circumstances may be.

The Shield of Faith—Then versus Now

The Roman soldier's shield, called a *scutum*, was a very large, slightly
curved wood, which was covered with animal skins and included a leather
strap on the inside for the soldier to grip. Boasting a size as large as four
feet by three feet with iron rims covering the sides, a Roman soldier's

shield resembled a door, sturdy and incredibly strong, with a large metal knob (called a *boss*—which is kind of perfect if you think about it) in the center of the shield.

Because of their impressive size, Roman shields afforded soldiers a great deal of protection from their enemies. The slight curve proved effective for deflecting attacks without transferring the full force of the assault onto the man holding the shield. The boss enabled a soldier to use his shield to deflect even the more vicious blows and functioned in a limited offensive capacity as a way to knock enemies backward.

Prior to battle, soldiers often dipped their shields in water so the enemy's flaming arrows were extinguished upon contact. The Roman army built a reputation as a fierce opponent with disciplined formations. A soldier would have held his shield in front of him (during close one-on-one combat) or overhead as a roof (in the *tortoise* formation), so a soldier was protected when he was alone, as well as when he battled with his brethren.

Think about a really bad day you have experienced. Maybe it started when you overslept and were late for school. You couldn't find your homework assignment for your first class, and your teacher said that no late submissions would be accepted. Then you stepped in gum on the way to lunch in your brand-new pair of Chuck Taylors that you saved for months to buy. You're pretty sure the note being passed during English was about you, and you are also fairly certain what was written on that little paper was full of unflattering things. Your favorite pen busted during your last class, which led you to add a ruined shirt to the list of all the other things that went wrong that day. When you got home from that awful day at school, both of your parents were there. They finally told you and your siblings what you've been dreading to hear: they're getting a divorce. It's the worst day ever.

When life circumstances feel like flaming arrows, and you are taking hit after hit after hit, this is when Paul instructs us: "In all circumstances take up the shield of faith, with which you can extinguish all the flaming darts of the evil one" (Eph. 6:16 ESV). This is when you need the most protection, because it is also when you are the most vulnerable.

What I shared in the previous chapter was not a bad day but rather a horrendous few weeks. Sometimes, battles last longer than a day, and think about how difficult it would be to sustain one-on-one combat for an extended period of time. Eventually, a soldier needs to duck and cover, taking protection beneath his shield. For Christians, this shield is our faith.

Saved by Faith

In the book of Esther, we learn about a beautiful young Jewish woman, Esther, who was married to a powerful Persian king named Xerxes. By this time in history, the Jews had been driven out of Israel and exiled in Persia. Since both of Esther's parents were dead, she was raised by her loving uncle, Mordecai, a Jewish official in King Xerxes's royal court. Esther was taken against her will from her uncle Mordecai's home at a fairly young age to live in the palace alongside other pretty girls from the city. Her beauty was renowned, and eventually King Xerxes named Esther the queen. Esther's Uncle Mordecai encouraged her to hide her faith from the King and his advisors, which she did.

King Xerxes was a pagan and did not believe in God, while Esther was a Jewish girl who was raised by her uncle to love and honor God. Uncle Mordecai found favor with King Xerxes when he overheard a plot of traitors who planned to kill the king and exposed their plan. However, King Xerxes's most powerful official, a man named Haman, did not like Mordecai because Mordecai refused to bow to him. Mordecai told Haman that he would only bow before God. When Ether's uncle refused the king's official, Mordecai made a powerful enemy.

In his pursuit of vengeance, Haman convinced King Xerxes to authorize a royal decree to annihilate the Jews. His evil plan was set into motion. Fortunately, Mordecai learned of Haman's plans, and he pleaded with his niece to intercede with her husband on behalf of the Jews.

Esther was afraid. Seeking an audience with her husband, the king, was delicate business. It was the custom in those days for no one to ever approach the king unless he summoned them first. To approach the king or request an audience could mean certain death! Queen Esther knew that asking to see her king was a dangerous mission, and she was surely afraid of how he might respond. However, Esther knew Haman's intentions were evil and agreed to help. She sent word back to her uncle that he and the other Jews should fast and pray for three days. Then, she requested her husband and Haman to join her for dinner two nights in a row.

On the night before the second banquet, the king had trouble sleeping. He ordered the book of chronicles, a record of his reign, to be brought to his chambers. It was marked to the page that recorded Mordecai's good deed when he had saved the king by exposing would-be assassins. When the king asked what reward had been given to Mordecai, his attendants told him that nothing had been done.

The next morning, just as Haman was coming to request Mordecai's execution, King Xerxes asked him, "What should I do for a man who truly pleases me?" Haman was a prideful man and mistakenly thought the king was referring to him. He replied by making an extravagant suggestion about how the king could honor a man. Haman had no sooner finished sharing this impressive list when the king ordered these actions to be carried out to honor none other than Mordecai.

Boy, was Haman in for a surprise! Imagine the king clapping his hands, exclaiming, "Excellent! Now, do just as you have said for Mordecai the Jew!" Haman was *un*happy, but he obeyed his king, albeit begrudgingly. Then, to add insult to injury, Haman still had to attend the second dinner with the king and queen.

It was then that Esther shared the secret of her faith and proclaimed herself a Jew. She begged her powerful husband to spare her people. One of the king's attendants also mentioned to the king that Haman had ordered gallows built to have Mordecai hanged. The king was furious with Haman and ordered the official's death instead. Esther's faith had saved her people.

Esther's circumstances were extreme, but we can learn a lot by her example of faith. Flip to Matthew 17:20 and read what it says about faith:

> Because you have so little faith. I tell you this: if you had even a faint spark of faith, even faith as tiny as a mustard seed, you could say to this mountain, "Move from here to there," and because of your faith, the mountain would move. If you had just a sliver of faith, you would find nothing impossible. (Matt. 17:20 *The Voice*)

Esther did not have the power to defeat her enemy, but she had faith that glorified God in a mighty way. While Satan stirred vengeance and hatred in Haman's heart, Esther leaned deeply into her shield of faith, trusting God to protect her and her people. Like Esther, when we have faith, we can defend against spiritual attacks that would try to separate us from God and dissuade us from believing his Word. And, like Haman, even though it makes Satan really, *really* mad, he has to obey his King as well. Have assurance in the knowledge that Satan is fully aware he is powerless to resist a command given in Jesus's name. This is why it is so important to speak aloud when rebuking the enemy and his attacks. Because when you command Satan in the name of Jesus, he *must* listen to you.

Living by Faith

We can learn much from men and women in the Bible who lived by faith. Match the biblical name or story with their act of faith:

1. Built an ark when there was no sign of rain (Gen. 6:9–22)

   Gideon

2. Healed a lame beggar by his faith in Jesus (Acts 3:1–16)

   Sinful woman

3. Slayed a huge giant in a battle with only five smooth river rocks (1 Sam. 17: 32–51)

   Criminal

4. Defeated an army of Midianites with only three hundred men (Judg. 7)

   Abraham

5. Was prepared to sacrifice his young son in obedience to God (Gen. 22)

6. Professed his faith next to Jesus on the cross (Luke 23:32–43)

   Joshua

7. Marched around Jericho for seven days, then played trumpets and shouted while the walls of the city crumbled down (Josh. 6:1–20)

   David

   Peter

8. Washed Jesus's feet with perfume and tears in thankfulness for forgiveness (Luke 7:35–50)

   Noah

Prepping Our Shields for Battle

Just like a Roman soldier would wet his shield before battle, we can "wet" our shields by engaging in activities that deepen our faith. Remember the enemy does have the power to make our lives pretty awful from time to time. However, the better we know God and the more time we spend with him, the tougher time Satan will have wounding us with a flaming arrow.

How do we build a relationship with God? God is relational, and he *wants* to spend time with you. You can deepen your relationship with God by:

- Reading God's Word
- Praying
- Worshiping
- Respecting God's authority
- Building community with other believers

The second you accepted Jesus as your Lord and Savior, the enemy set his sights on you. It's no surprise Satan begins his fiery assault when we take our first steps in faith. Remember his ultimate battle objective is to separate Christians from God and keep those who do not know Jesus yet from receiving the gift of salvation. The enemy's flaming arrows come from many angles and carry poisons like insecurity, doubt, shame, anxiety, depression, and more.

Take a minute to look up the following verses and write them in the following spaces:

1 Timothy 6:12

James 4:8

Psalm 145:18–19

Jeremiah 29:11–13

Even in the midst of a fierce battle, God has not left you defenseless. Even on your very worst day, you are not alone. God meets us in the midst of our furnaces, just like he met Shadrach, Meshach, and Abednego. Fear not, for God has redeemed you and called you by name (Isa. 43:1). You have the authority in Jesus's name to shut the enemy down and walk forward in faith without fear.

Your community is another layer of defense (remember your *tortoise* formation). Lean into your community and let them walk with you. Soak yourself in God's Word and keep your shield wet with Scripture. The Living Water on your shield not only deflects Satan's flaming arrows; it snuffs them out completely. Rest in the confidence of God's promises, because he will never abandon you to your circumstances and leave you to battle alone.

An Activity for Parents and Tweens:
Armor Design—Shield of Faith

This week, work on constructing your own shield of faith. Remember we are working on building our own personal armor to prepare for the messy, entertaining battle coming at the end of this study!

Use materials you have lying around the house for an extra challenge. This is an activity that fits within any budget, so be creative and have fun!

As you work on your shields this week, discuss the relational nature of God. How might you individually spend time with him? What distractions keep you from doing so, and how might you address them? Think of some activities you can do as a family to better prepare for your own *tortoise* formation. When one of you needs help and feels the sting of Satan's arrow, how will your family rally around one another? Talk about your family battle plan.

In my house, we call family meetings and take turns praying aloud over one another. We commit to praying for one another by name in our own quiet times with God. We pray Scripture over one another. Brainstorm as a family and decide how your family will respond when a family member is under spiritual attack.

Take a few minutes to hold hands and pray aloud. Thank God for his caring nature, and ask him to reveal more relational characteristics to you. If you are uncomfortable coming up with your own prayer, try the one provided below.

Heavenly Father,

In your infinite wisdom, you crafted the perfect armor to defend against an enemy who never slumbers or sleeps. Thank you for your provision against his attacks, Lord. Help me to take up my faith when I feel the heat of Satan's flaming arrows drawing close, and help me to trust Jesus when one or more of those arrows wounds me or someone I love.

Forgive me in moments of weakness, Lord, when I choose to retreat from battle instead of trusting you to meet me in the middle of it. In all things, I choose you. Help my life choices reflect and honor you in all I do.

I know you waste nothing, Father. Please use my circumstances to show another who may not know you what it means to take up the shield of faith, to trust you no matter what is happening and no matter how awful or awesome my day has been. Use my life as a testimony to your goodness and faithfulness. I am so honored to serve you, God.

In Jesus's precious name I pray,
Amen.

Calling Workshop Apprentices!
Project: Shield of Faith

Materials needed:

- Cardboard (can use old mailing boxes)
- Poster board
- Masking or duct tape
- Scissors or box cutter
- Craft paint
- Glue stick or hot glue

Note: You will need some pretty good-sized pieces of cardboard. If you do not have any on hand, pop by your local grocery or home store. These types of businesses usually have plenty of used boxes that get tossed into the trash.

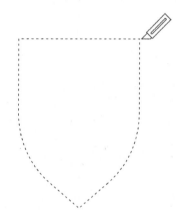

Step 1: Using the template in the Appendix, outline the shape of your shield on the cardboard and poster board. Then use scissors or a box cutter to cut the shields out.

Step 2: Grab your paints and cover the front of your cardboard and poster board.

Step 3: While your paint is drying, cut a rectangular piece of cardboard that is same the width as your shield. Attach the new piece to the back of the shield using duct or masking tape. This will become the support for the handles on the back of the shield.

Step 4: With your remaining pieces of cardboard, cut (2) 10-inch by 2-inch strips, which you will secure to the back of the shield. These handles become your arm/hand holds for the back of the shield.

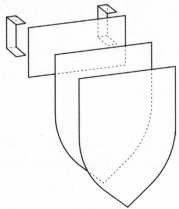

Step 5: Tape the handles down firmly using duct or masking tape.

Step 6: Glue the decorated poster board to the front of your shield. Trim the edges as needed. This is your shield, so personalize and make it your own! You may want to use poster board to create your own Coat of Arms or a cross. Use your imagination, and have fun!

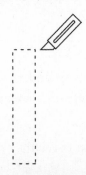

What's Your
SITREP?

It's time for a situation report, so let's check your understanding and dig deeper into the context of Chapter Five.

1. What does it mean to have faith? (*Hint*: Look back at Hebrew 11:1 and write it in the space below, along with your own thoughts about what it means to have faith.) Does your own definition of faith differ from what you see in this passage? If yes, how so?

2. Read Exodus 11:4–6, 12:5–13. How did the people of Israel show faith in God? How did God respond to their demonstration of obedience and trust?

3. Do you trust God and believe his Word?

4. Sometimes people say one thing but their actions do not match their words. This is a tough question, but think and respond honestly. Is the risk to follow Jesus in today's culture worth it when Christianity is not necessarily the popular thing to do?

5. How does Satan distract you with his flaming arrows?

6. If you had to give each of the enemy's arrows a name, what would they be (discouragement, doubt, anger, etc.)?

7. Do you think the enemy uses fear to keep you from stepping in faith? Talk about this with your mom or dad.

8. Look up Luke 17:5–6 and write it in the space below. Have you ever felt like you needed more faith? Remember all of the examples you read in this chapter about people walking in faith and remember how big God is.

9. It's time to put yourself into the story. Read 1 Samuel 17:33–51. Imagine what it would have been like to be David. Perhaps even replace David's name with your own. Talk with your parent(s) about what this experience might have felt like for a young boy or girl facing a battle-hardened soldier with only a slingshot and five river rocks.

10. Are there flaming arrows in your shield that have yet to be extinguished? Take time now to pray that God will snuff out the fire and push the enemy back.

THIS WEEK'S **BATTLE PLAN**

1. Pray and ask God to give you clear insight as to how the enemy is distracting you from stepping forward in faith. Write things down or talk with mom or dad about what you discover, and then pray together to remove those fiery darts from your shield of faith. This exercise should take some time, so try to set aside a quiet time each day this week to devote to listening and receiving what God is saying to you. *Battle tactic: The closer you are to God, the more difficult it will be for the enemy to separate you. Keep your shield of faith wet in preparation for Satan's flaming arrows, so they will be extinguished on contact.*

2. Continue to pray the armor of God over yourself and each member of your family.

Letters from the Battlefield

Dear Friend,

Sitting in the stuffy classroom, I looked up from my geometry review when a pair of voices called my name. Two of my fellow freshmen, Evan and Sarah, beckoned me over. I knew Sarah from church, while Evan and I had met through our geometry class. As I approached the pair, Evan asked me if I was a Christian. "Yes, I am," I responded as I tentatively approached the table. "You actually believe that there's a God?" Evan groaned, irritation palpable in his voice. "Yes, I do," I answered cautiously. Sarah informed me that she and Evan had been debating the factual basis of Christianity. Since Sarah knew me from church, she thought that my perspective would be a valuable asset to their discussion.

As a freshman fresh out of a private Christian middle school, the conversation I was about to enter was not unexpected. I had been told time and time again that high school would be a battleground filled with classmates ready to attack my faith. I prepared accordingly, arming myself with Bible verses, praying constantly, and devouring the lessons from my religion classes. Still, here was a boy who was armed with the fiery arrows of doubt and deception that the Lord warns us about, and despite my preparation, I had never felt more afraid.

Nevertheless, I said a quick prayer and stood my ground, bringing up several rational explanations that validated my case. I confidently marched forward, speaking truth and standing firm in it. Despite this, Evan brought up unsettling points and facts that had never crossed my

mind. For every one of my justifications, Evan had a line
of reasoning that knocked mine to the ground. I became
frustrated as every time I tried to speak, Evan would
brush off my arguments as irrational or naïve. Suddenly,
the bell rang, and I felt tears well up in my eyes. As Evan
walked out of the classroom, I felt that I had let my
friend, myself, and my God down.

Jesus tells us directly that "[i]n this world, you will
have trouble" (John 16:33 NIV) and that "because you are
not of the world . . . the world [will hate] you" (John
15:19 ESV). After my debate with Evan, I had never felt the
truth of these verses more prominently. I felt bruised
and broken as the devil's arrows begged to plant doubt
in my soul. Yet the lying arrows extinguished around me,
failing to penetrate my heart, as my shield of faith consumed their fiery touch.

In 2 Corinthians 4:16-18, Paul tells us,

Do not lose heart. Though our outer self is
wasting away, our inner self is being renewed day by
day. For this light momentary affliction is preparing
for us an eternal weight of glory beyond all comparison, as we look not to the things that are seen
but to the things that are unseen. For the things
that are seen are transient, but the things that are
unseen are eternal. (ESV)

Paul was a seasoned sufferer. He had been whipped,
beaten, imprisoned, and gone hungry, all because of his
faith in Christ. It would have been easy for him to
rebuke his faith and end the suffering. Instead, he took
up his shield of faith, spread the good news, and wrote

that our "light momentary affliction is preparing for us an eternal weight of glory."

Throughout the Bible, we can see the fruit that comes from having faith. Mary, who was only a teenager, had faith in God and was able to give birth to our Lord and Savior Jesus Christ. Noah was ridiculed for building the ark, yet his faith in God enabled him to save his family and all of God's creatures from the flood. Moses, although afraid, had faith in God and freed the Israelites from slavery.

Even though Evan had fired arrows of fear, doubt, hopelessness, and despair, my shield stood firm against his fire. Furthermore, I realized that I was not alone. Sarah was beside me the entire time, and since that day, we have become best friends. My encounter inspired me to become the president of my high school's Fellowship of Christian Athletes chapter so that I could build a community with fellow believers as well as reach classmates like Evan. Although the experience tested my beliefs, my shield of faith protected me from listening to Satan's lies and inspired me to dive into my faith in ways I could have never imagined.

Friend, I encourage you to take up your shield no matter how overwhelming the circumstances may be. God does not ask for perfect people but rather for those who are willing to have faith in him. Know that you are beautiful, cherished, and loved beyond measure. I know that God will do amazing things through you. All it takes is a little faith.

With Love,
Victoria

Dear Friend,

I grew up completely surrounded by my faith in a private school up until high school, when I switched to a public school. In some ways, it was hard to transition to this kind of a school, but in others, it really wasn't. For example, I was blessed in that most of my friends who had gone to my old school and church would be attending the same high school with me as well. These people have made a true impact on who I am today and how I view right from wrong. See, if I had gone into this school alone, I know it would have been a different journey to the moral standards I hold close today. Since I attended a private school for the majority of my life, I was constantly surrounded by people reinforcing this idea of what is right and how we should hold ourselves to such things each and every day.

When I transitioned to public school, this was different, as I now had to intentionally seek out reminders of how the life I was choosing to lead was right in God's eyes. I consciously held my faith as a shield to reject the idea that I needed to participate in worldly things like drinking or partying every night (like many of my teammates did) in order to be satisfied. Not every experience is like mine, where there is a close group of people with you every step of the way. This made transitioning to a public school a little easier for me. One of the harder things to do was holding up my shield of faith and not falling prey to the social temptations and daily acts of unkindness and sin, like cursing or being rude to people in the hallways.

In my previous school, they taught that being kind is the only way to be and it is the right way to act. One thing that my private school didn't prepare me well for was facing people whose definition of what's right, moral, and kind was totally different from how I was raised to believe God wants us to act. This new reality was a huge shock to me. Now, as a senior, it is almost as if I have become immune to the effects these sins have on me. They aren't as much of a shock anymore, which in and of itself seems okay in that I'm just used to them. However, I have accepted this new reality as something that happens daily, because it just is. I have grown accustomed to what is seen as plausible or right in the minds of the public and, for most of my school, non-Christians. Awareness does not mean acceptance, though.

What I encourage you to do is to hold fast to your shield of faith when you feel surrounded by the temptation of sin. Seek what is "right" in God's eyes, and try to find people to help hold you accountable, as my friends have done for me all of these years. Yes, it can be tough to resist the enemy's cleverly masked temptations of sin, and no one is perfect. However, this community of people that I have been surrounded with has helped me time and time again when I fall short and make a mistake. They gently remind me that even though I am not perfect, God loves me so much.

I also encourage you to be a light. Strive to make choices that honor God and the person he is calling you to be. Be a source of encouragement and strive to love one another, even when those around you aren't loving or kind in return. It will be tough, but just know that you are not alone in your struggle. Remember to lean on God's truth, and never be ashamed to lead your life like he would want you to lead it.

Sincerely,
Emily

Chapter Six

The Helmet
of Salvation

*If you openly declare that Jesus is Lord and believe in your heart
that God raised him from the dead, you will be saved. For it is
by believing in your heart that you are made right with God,
and it is by openly declaring your faith that you are saved.*

Romans 10:9–10 (NLT)

Acquitted!

In Ephesians 6:17, Paul tells us to "take the helmet of salvation" (NIV). By
now, we understand that salvation comes through Jesus—for he is the
way, the truth, and the life (John 14:6). The word *salvation* comes from
the Greek word *soteria*, which means to save, to deliver, to set free. Before
knowing Jesus and accepting him as our Lord and Savior, we were under
the power of sin.

> So the trouble is not with the law, for it is spiritual and good.
> The trouble is with me, for I am all too human, a slave to
> sin. . . . And I know that nothing good lives in me, that is,
> in my sinful nature. I want to do what is right, but I can't. I
> want to do what is good, but I don't. I don't want to do what
> is wrong, but I do it anyway. But if I do what I don't want to
> do, I am not really the one doing wrong; it is sin living in me
> that does it. (Rom. 7:14, 18–20 NLT)

There are some who believe that people are not innately sinful. Some people even believe there is no such thing as sin. If that were true, there would be no need for a Savior. Remember, mankind broke fellowship with God in the Garden of Eden when Adam and Eve disobeyed and ate the forbidden fruit. Since then, it's been a constant back-and-forth as we have tried to reestablish fellowship with God. Even God's chosen people, the Israelites, have a history of running from him. The Old Testament is full of examples of Israel straying from the path of righteousness, God delivering and forgiving them, and the Israelites rejoicing. Then before you know it, there the Israelites go again.

We are no different. We are just as inclined to wander and stray from God as the Israelites were. Yet God still comes to rescue us. The only difference is the method we use to atone or justify our sins, which is a legal term signifying *acquittal*. In the days of the Old Testament, God gave the Israelites a process for atonement that was performed by a high priest to absolve them of their sins. A blood sacrifice was required. The price of sin is death. Period. That might seem extreme, but the problem isn't the law. As Romans 7:14, 18–20, says, the problem is our human nature. As sinners, we owe a debt we could never repay.

This is what makes the story of salvation such good news! God sent his perfect Son to earth so that we could be justified or made right as the law demanded. Jesus paid the blood price, and we were acquitted or *freed* from having to pay the debt we owe for our sins.

Armor with a Purpose

God's provision of a spiritual helmet is essential in the unseen war. When a soldier is on the battlefield, a head wound is serious business. Guarding our minds is just as important as guarding our hearts. Just as the breastplate of righteousness protects the heart, one of our most vital organs, the helmet of salvation protects the head. The hope of salvation is represented as a helmet. Yet hope isn't used in the sense of wishful thinking; rather, it is used in the sense of a confident expectation of God's hand in the future. Remember when Shadrach, Meshach, and Abednego were thrown into the fiery furnace? God did not abandon them to their circumstances, just like he does not abandon us to ours. We can confidently trust that God meets us and walks with us in the present moment, regardless of whether we are delivered from our trials.

> But let us who live in the light be clearheaded, protected by the armor of faith and love, and wearing as our helmet the confidence of our salvation. (1 Thess. 5:8 NLT)

10,000 Talents

Let's take a look at the following passage from Matthew 18:23–27 (NLT):

> Therefore, the Kingdom of Heaven can be compared to a king who decided to bring his accounts up to date with servants who had borrowed money from him. In the process, one of his debtors was brought in who owed him millions of dollars. He couldn't pay, so his master ordered that he be sold—along with his wife, his children, and everything he owned—to pay the debt. But the man fell down before his master and begged him, "Please, be patient with me, and I will pay it all." Then his master was filled with pity for him, and he released him and forgave his debt.

This story is about a servant who owed his master ten thousand talents. It would have taken the servant fifteen years to repay just one talent, so in essence, he could never justify this debt with his master! The master had the right to sell the man and his children as slaves in order to satisfy the debt, but the master chose to cancel and forgive the debt instead. The servant did not have to pay what he rightly owed.

Think about the debt of sin we have to God. It is so heavy and oppressive that we could never repay God what we owe. The only way for us to be justified before God is for him to cancel and forgive our debt. Friends, this is *exactly* what God has done for each of us! When Jesus died on the cross, he took our sins with him.

Before and After Salvation

Look up the following verses and decide if the passage reflects life *before* salvation or *after*.

Bible Passage	Before Salvation	After Salvation
Titus 3:3–7		
Romans 8:6–8		
1 Corinthians 2:14		
Proverbs 14:12		
Romans 13:14		
Galatians 5:16–17		
Colossians 1:21		
Jeremiah 17:9		
Titus 1:15		
Romans 8:38–39		

Have you accepted Jesus as your Lord and Savior and put on your helmet of salvation? If you haven't and would like to do that today, ask your mom or dad to pray with you right now.

God Sent Jesus for YOU

Take a peek at Psalm 139:13–16 (NLT):

> You made all the delicate, inner parts of my body
>   and knit me together in my mother's womb.
> Thank you for making me so wonderfully complex!
>   Your workmanship is marvelous—how well I know it.
> You watched me as I was being formed in utter seclusion,
>   as I was woven together in the dark of the womb.
> You saw me before I was born.
>   Every day of my life was recorded in your book.
> Every moment was laid out
>   before a single day had passed.

You are part of God's plan. Way before you drew your first earthly breath, God already loved you. Look at the care with which Scripture tells us that God knit us together in our mothers' wombs. The father of lies constantly whispers in your ear that you are unloved, unworthy, unseen, and this is *false*. The great I Am loves you, finds you worthy, and sees you better than anyone else.

The Helmet of Salvation—Then versus Now

The Roman helmet, known as a *galea*, was made of brass or bronze and lined with felt. The most obvious value of the helmet was to protect against blows to the head, which would have immediately knocked a soldier out of battle. A soldier's helmet usually had cheek plates to guard against blows to the face and a metal piece in the back to protect against blows to the back of the neck. Even though it was technically the last piece of body armor a soldier strapped onto his body, he could not engage in combat without it.

As Christians, Paul tells us to "put on the helmet of salvation" (Eph. 6:17). Without it, we leave ourselves exposed on the spiritual battlefield. Much like the Roman soldier's helmet protected his brain, which we know is central to controlling the movement of the body and unconscious functions like breathing, the helmet of salvation protects our minds. How we think determines predominantly how we act, and a well-guarded mind helps us stand firm against the schemes of the devil.

> Do not allow this world to mold you in its own image. Instead, be transformed from the inside out by renewing your mind. As a result, you will be able to discern what God wills and whatever God finds good, pleasing, and complete. (Rom. 12:2 *The Voice*)

So how do we put on the helmet of salvation if we already have salvation? Salvation comes from Jesus, and once you have invited him into your heart, he resides there permanently. The devil cannot kick him out. Rather, putting on the helmet of salvation is a conscious decision to place your hope in the salvation of Jesus. Satan plagues us with doubts about our salvation, whispers worldly ideas and wants in our ears, and would have us focus on the now instead of eternity. This is what Paul means when he talks about the *renewal* of our minds in Romans 12:2. If we allow the enemy's seeds of doubt to take root in our minds, he lands a blow to the head, and then we spend less time spreading the gospel because we are too busy nursing our own head wounds.

Each day is a new day on the spiritual battlefield, which means spending a few minutes in the morning praying the armor of God over yourself and your loved ones. Remember the worst day you ever experienced. Satan uses awful tragedies around the world, he plants doubts daily, and he wants us to worry over the loss of our salvation. However, it is in times like these that we need to *renew our trust* in the Lord. If it helps, physically put your hands on your head as you bow your face and ask God to restore your hope, rebuking the enemy's attack.

When you invited Jesus into your heart, you were adopted into God's family. That adoption is permanent and unbreakable. Amen and amen, right?

An Activity for Parents and Tweens:
Armor Design—Helmet of Salvation

This week, work on constructing your own helmet of salvation. Remember we are working on building our own personal armor to prepare for the messy, entertaining battle coming at the end of this study!

Use materials you have lying around the house for an extra challenge. This is an activity that fits within any budget, so be creative and have fun!

While you're working this week, recall a really awful day you've had. Walk back through the day and look for moments for which you can be thankful. For example, let's consider the following experience:

Think back to a day when you overslept and were late for school. (The spirit of frustration was present.) Yet, that morning, you woke up in a warm bed, with a roof over your head and food in the pantry. You live in a place where you can attend school, even if you have to attend class online rather than in person. School is still accessible. For that, you can be thankful.

You couldn't find your homework assignment for your first class, and your teacher said no late submissions would be accepted. (The spirit of unworthiness was present.) The same teacher gently reminded you that she drops the lowest score and that while she cannot give you credit for the work that is missing, she can assure you that your grade will not be affected as long as you turn in the rest of your assignments. For that, you can be thankful.

Then, you stepped in gum on the way to lunch in your brand-new pair of Chuck Taylors that you saved for months to buy. (The spirit of anger and desolation was present.) Even though it took part of your lunch period, you were able to scrub the gum off your shoe in the bathroom. No permanent damage was done. For that, you can be thankful.

You're pretty sure the note being passed during English was about you, and you are also fairly certain what was written on that little paper was full of unflattering things. (The spirit of unworthiness was present *again*.) Your best friend has the same class with you, and she gave you a reassuring hug after class. You were hurt, but you were not alone. Your friend always has your back. For that, you can be thankful.

Your favorite pen busted during your last class, and now you can add a ruined shirt to all the other things that went wrong that day. (The spirits of shame and embarrassment were present.) At least it was the last class of the day, and no one seemed to notice the interesting pattern on your otherwise rather plain T-shirt. Even if you can never wear this shirt to school again, you have plenty of other shirts hanging in your closet. For that, you can be thankful.

When you get home from that awful day at school, both of your parents are there. They finally tell you and your siblings what you've been dreading to hear: they're getting a divorce. (The spirit of sadness was present.) Your parents haven't been happy for a long time, but you still can't muster up thankfulness for their divorce. However, your dad moved out but he only moved fifteen minutes away. You and your siblings still get to spend time with both parents, and your mom and dad seem to be getting along better than they have in as long as you can remember. You still feel sad that your parents aren't together, but this situation seems to be healthier for everyone. For that, you can be thankful.

It was the worst day ever—or so the enemy made you believe. Yet God did not abandon you to those awful circumstances. He met you in the blazing furnace you found yourself facing that day. In the cracks and spaces between those horrible moments were reaffirming ones—sweet and tender reminders by God that you are worthy, you are loved, and you are seen.

Spend some time in prayer together this week, thanking God for those special *winks* on days when the spiritual war is raging and you feel beaten down. Try the prewritten prayer below if you have trouble coming up with your own.

Dear Loving Father,

Thank you for saving me, Abba. Even when Satan is determined to make me believe I am alone, I know you never abandon me. Thank you for those special glimpses into your deep and abiding love, especially on the days when tough moments outweigh the easy ones. Thank you for all the blessings you give me, but most importantly, thank you for the gift of Jesus.

When the enemy begins to whisper lies that make me want to doubt my faith, help me put on my helmet of salvation. Help me to remember the forgiveness of my sins and the gift of eternity with you is something that Satan can never take away from me. In those moments, help me lean deeper into you, God. Tuck me close and give me rest from the onslaught of the enemy's blows to my head and assault on my mind.

I love you, Father God.

In your Son's perfect name, I pray,
Amen.

Calling Workshop Apprentices!
Project: Helmet of Salvation

Materials needed:

- Cardboard (can use old mailing boxes)
- Glue or masking/duct tape
- Sharpie
- Exacto knife or scissors
- Tape measure
- Markers or spray paint (if desired)

Step 1: Measure the soldier's head. Add a couple of inches to the measurement. Mark the length needed (soldier's head + 2 inches) by 2 inches wide with a Sharpie onto the cardboard. You will need three straps total.

Step 2: Once you have the outline of your straps, use an Exacto knife or scissors to cut them out.

Step 3: Bend the strap until it makes a ring. Overlap the ends by one inch. Then secure the two sides together with glue or tape.

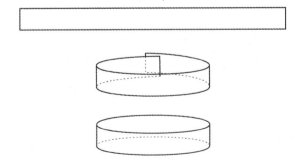

Step 4: Take one of the other straps and attach one side to the outside of the first ring. Secure with glue or masking tape. Attach the other side of the new strap to the opposite outer side of the ring.

Step 5: Take the third strap and attached so that the two top straps criss-cross over the top of the ring.

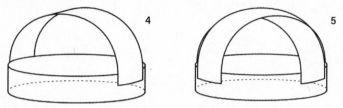

Step 6: Measure and cut half circles of cardboard to fill in the gaps on the helmet. Use glue or masking tape to secure.

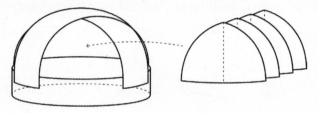

Step 7: Using a measuring tape, measure the length of the helmet from front to back. Using the template in the Appendix as a guide for your helmet plume, mark your outline with the correct length on your cardboard.

Step 8: Then cut out and adjust as needed to your helmet. Once the fitting is the way you want it, cut the outer edge of the cardboard (not cutting completely through to the other side), giving the plume a feathered look.

Step 9: Secure the plume with glue or tape.

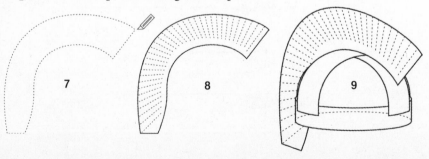

Step 10: Using the template in the Appendix, use a Sharpie to draw the face guard for your helmet. Cut out with an Exacto knife or box cutter (*adult supervision required*).

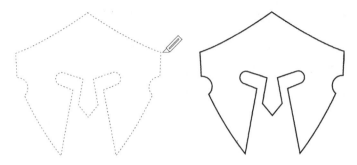

Step 11: Attached the face guard to the front of your helmet with tape or glue. Then decorate your helmet with spray paint and/or markers. Your helmet should now be battle ready!

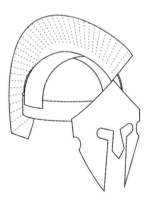

What's Your
SITREP?

It's time for a situation report, so let's check your understanding and dig deeper into the context of Chapter Six.

1. Look up Colossians 1:13–14 and copy it down in the space below. How does this describe the world?

2. Read Matthew 22:35–38. What does it mean to love the Lord with your mind? Now read Romans 8:5–11. Talk with your parent(s) about the difference of living by the ways of the world (the ways the flesh desires) and the ways of the Word (the ways the Spirit desires).

3. Read Titus 3:3–7. What were we like before God saved us? Did God save us because of our good deeds or because of his mercy? What hope is ours now?

4. How would you describe your personal story of salvation?

5. Write down obstacles that keep you from sharing your story with others.

6. Knowing you have the authority to rebuke the enemy in Jesus's name, what can you do to remove the obstacles you wrote down above?

7. Is there sin weighing on your mind? Look up Ephesians 1:7 and read it aloud. Now personalize this passage with your name: "In him, I, (your name), have redemption through his blood, the forgiveness of sins, in accordance with the riches of God's grace." Pray with your mom or dad and ask God to forgive the sin you need to confess, and then trust in God and the redemptive power of Jesus's sacrifice that you have been set free.

8. Look up Ephesians 1:3–6. What does it say about when God decided to adopt us into his family? How long has he known and loved us?

9. Look up Ephesians 2:8–9 and write it in the space below. Why is this passage good news?

THIS WEEK'S **BATTLE PLAN**

1. Sharing the good news of Jesus can be intimidating, especially in a culture that does not always support Christians. This week, practice sharing your testimony. Talk with your parent(s) about how you might share your story and the good news of Jesus with others. *Battle tactic: A soldier does not enter the battlefield unprepared. He trains and practices. The more you practice sharing your own story of salvation, the more prepared you will be and the more confident you will feel! Remember that for people who do not know Jesus, yours is the first face of faith they may see.*

2. Pray and ask God to place the name or names of people who need to hear your story on your heart.

Letters from the Battlefield

Dear Friend,

One thing I wish I would have known when I was younger was that it's okay not to understand everything about God in order to accept his gift of salvation. While I remember praying a prayer asking Jesus to forgive me of my sin when I was very young, I consider my salvation story to be more of a gradual understanding than a one-time moment. It started when I began to understand what sin was, that my sin separated me from God, and that I needed Jesus to save me. I remember asking God to save me, and I know he did, but I still had so many questions. For years, I struggled with those questions, thinking that I needed to understand everything about God and his ways in order to be saved. But over time I've finally started to realize that it's okay to not know all of the answers, and it's even okay to wrestle with God over things—maybe that's why Jacob wrestling with God in Genesis is one of my favorite Bible stories.

I think God actually likes when we ask questions, because we are trying to get to know him better. And while he does reveal a lot to us, and gives us many answers, a lot of times he doesn't, which means we have to learn to be content in not knowing. That's still hard for me, but I'm getting there, because thankfully my salvation is not based on my understanding all the ways of God, but on his power and ability to save me.

So if you feel like you have more questions than answers, don't worry. You can still receive God's gift of salvation. And then you can begin a great adventure of getting to know him more.

In Him,
Andrew

~~~

Dear Friend,

For the first sixteen years of my life, I wasn't Christian. During this time, I wasn't ignoring God, but I didn't exactly know anything about who he was or have a relationship with him. My salvation story started a little later compared to most people around me, which was very intimidating at first, as I was stepping into a life I knew nothing about. What I didn't know is that God was always at work even during the trials, tears, panic attacks, and whatever lies the enemy tried to discourage me with.

Throughout my whole life, God had been sowing little seeds in me until I came to fully accept Christ in a small church in the Dominican Republic. Looking back now, I can't exactly remember what prompted me to apply for a mission trip through a church I hadn't even attended regularly. I really only knew one other person who attended it. Despite all of the unknowns, I signed up to go on my very first mission trip to the Dominican Republic. During all the months of training sessions leading up to the trip, I was paralyzed by fear because I felt unworthy and underqualified to be used by God. I was diving into a world and community I felt that I wasn't _enough_ for, and I was too scared to even pray out loud.

The purpose of our mission trip was to partner with a local church to share the life-changing reality of Jesus Christ in areas that had not heard the gospel, primarily through backyard Bible clubs. During the backyard Bible clubs, we danced with the kids, put on skits about Jesus, and at the end of the gospel presentation, we asked anyone who felt led to come up and accept Jesus Christ as their Lord and Savior. Each day I sat back and watched little kids slowly walk up to the altar to accept Jesus. Suddenly, it dawned on me that I had never done that. Sure, I had started attending church, highlighting verses in my Bible and raising my hands during worship, but I couldn't remember when I had prayed to accept Jesus. On the day of our third backyard Bible club, I was sitting on the ground with the kids, and when one of my team members invited people up to the altar, I slowly stood and made what felt like the longest walk of my life to the front of the church. It was there in a remote town in the Dominican Republic, surrounded by kids who I had just met, that I gave my life to Christ.

When I returned home, I took all the lessons God taught me in the Dominican Republic and felt the weight of my sin slowly lift off of me. After my salvation, I realized that most of the frustrations and failures I had experienced in my B.C. (before Christ) life had come from me believing Satan's lies that I am unloved, that I am not good enough, and that I am unworthy of this life God has given me. What I have come to realize from walking with God is that he doesn't always call the influential, noble, or qualified in this world (1 Cor. 1:26-31); he uses ordinary people to achieve his purpose. Unfortunately, choosing God's ways is not always easy. There will be days when you start to believe Satan's lies, but you will feel better when you take your eyes off the enemy's lies and refocus them on God. Always remember that he is above all your problems, pain, and swirling moments of this life, and you can rest knowing that "God is our refuge and strength, an ever-present help in trouble" (Ps. 46:1-3). May you live every day expressing confidence in the faithfulness of who he is and who he has called you to be.

In wonder with love,
Juju

Chapter Seven

The Sword
of the Spirit

All of Scripture is God-breathed; in its inspired voice, we hear
useful teaching, rebuke, correction, instruction, and training
for a life that is right so that God's people may be up to the task
ahead and have all they need to accomplish every good work.

2 Timothy 3:16–17 (*The Voice*)

The Power of the Spoken Word

This is a topic I have been passionate about through many years of Bible study with parents and their tweens. Words hold *immense* power. Any person can likely recall words that have stuck in their spirit, whether those words were imparted kindly or hurtfully. That old adage of "sticks and stones may break my bones but words can never hurt me" is a *complete* lie.

We bear the image of our Creator, who literally spoke our world into being.

> And God said, "Let there be light," and there was light.
> (Gen. 1:3 ESV)

As an image bearer of the very God who created the heavens and the earth (Gen. 1:26–28), you better believe your words hold power, too. No word we speak is without significance. Take a minute to look up the following verses and write them in the following spaces:

1 Corinthians 14:10

Matthew 12:36–37

We know words have great significance. Look where the Bible even compares the tongue to a sword:

> I am surrounded by fierce lions
> who greedily devour human prey—
> whose teeth pierce like spears and arrows,
> and whose tongues cut like swords. (Ps. 57:4 NLT)

> They sharpen their tongues like swords
> and aim cruel words like deadly arrows. (Ps. 64:3 NIV)

> There is one whose rash words are like sword thrusts,
> but the tongue of the wise brings healing. (Prov. 12:18 ESV)

Then in John 15:7, we learn what happens when we use our mouths to speak the most powerful words—the Word of God. It says, "If you abide in me, and my words abide in you, ask whatever you wish, and it will be done for you" (ESV).

That is why the last piece of our spiritual armor is so essential. It is the only offensive weapon we have against the enemy. In Ephesians 6:17, Paul instructs us to take up "the sword of the Spirit, which is the word of God" (NIV).

Tapping into the Power of the Word

The apostle John tells us, "In the beginning was the Word, and the Word was with God, and the Word was God" (John 1:1 NIV). Look a little closer at the first chapter of John at verse 14: "So the Word became human and made his home among us. He was full of unfailing love and faithfulness.

And we have seen his glory, the glory of the Father's one and only Son" (John 1:14 NLT).

I love this. John was so clever in his writing. The Greek translation of *word* in this passage is *logos*, which was commonly used in both Greek and Jewish biblical cultures. Greek philosophers used the word *logos* to describe God at the beginning of creation—a force that created the cosmos out of nothingness and gave it order, form, and meaning. By introducing Jesus as the Word, John draws upon a familiar term and concept that both Gentiles and Jews of his day would have been familiar with. Just like Jesus used parables to teach, John finds familiar ground so the good news is instantly relatable and understood by the people who need to receive the message of salvation.

John introduces Jesus as the *logos*, personalizing the Old Testament God, creator of the universe. John describes Jesus Christ as the Word (see also Rev. 19:13), and he further explains that Jesus, the Word, became a man to bear witness to the truth (John 18:37). Jesus is the Truth (John 14:6)—the personification of the written and spoken Word. In the Old Testament, God revealed his Word through prophets like Elijah, Isaiah, and Haggai. In the New Testament, the Word of God is revealed in a Person, and that Person is Jesus Christ, the Son of God. And Jesus performed miracles, yes, but the primary way he spread his teachings was through the use of his spoken words.

Yet the Word is not only reflected in the Person of Jesus Christ; it is also reflected in the written Word of God—the Bible. We know all of Scripture is God-breathed (2 Tim. 3:16–17). Even though Jesus's life and teachings are only represented in part of the Bible, it is all divinely inspired. This is why the spoken Word of God is so incredibly powerful. When you spend time in the Word of God, you are tapping into the power of *Logos*, which is the power of Jesus Christ, the power of God.[1]

When you look up a word in the English dictionary, you might see that some words actually have multiple meanings. The same is true of the Greek terminology for *word*. In Greek, there are actually three different uses:

Graphe—The written word; in terms of the Bible, what God
    instructed other people to write down.

Logos—The active and living message of the writing, like John using
   Word or *Logos* to explain the gift of salvation.
Rhema—The spoken word.

In Ephesians 6:17, Paul is talking about a different meaning of the *word*
than John used. Paul uses *rhema* for the spoken word. He is instructing
us to use the Word of God against Satan and his evil schemes. In essence,
when we leave our words unspoken, we leave our swords in their sheaths!

Weapon Bearer, Skilled Swordsman, or Bible Ninja

Take the following quiz to find out what your skill level is!

1. When I feel overwhelmed by my terrible, awful day, I:

   a. Take a nap, because today has been utterly exhausting.

   b. Ask my parent or someone else I trust to pray for me.

   c. Open my Bible and begin to read Scripture aloud.

2. In my head, a voice keeps telling me how stupid I am, so I:

   a. Try to focus on my homework instead.

   b. Take my mind off of my thoughts by spending time with a
      good friend.

   c. Stop for a minute and pray aloud, asking God to replace the
      lie I hear with his truth.

3. My parents just broke the news that they are getting a divorce. I:

   a. Lose my cool *completely*. I mean, are they even thinking
      about anyone besides themselves?

   b. FaceTime my best friend. After all, her parents have already
      been through this, and I know she will have good advice
      for me.

   c. Pray that God sees my family through this tough time.

4. My sister came into my room without asking and accidentally broke my brand-new phone. I:

    a. Retaliate, because she has destroyed my property for the last time.

    b. Tell my parents immediately and ask them to intervene.

    c. Take a breath. It was an accident, and our parents will likely make her help pay for the damages. She already feels terrible, so I forgive her and tell her it will be okay.

5. My friend forgot my birthday, but he can't stop talking about the invitation he received to another party . . . which happens to be the same night he was supposed to be celebrating with me. I:

    a. Distance myself; we can no longer be friends because he clearly doesn't care about me.

    b. Decide not to say anything. I'll get over it eventually, and I don't want my friend to be mad at me.

    c. Pray before confronting my friend in a loving way. I want to be honest about how his actions hurt me, because our friendship is important.

6. My mom forgot to pick me up from school . . . *again*. This is the third time this month. I:

    a. Cry and lament to my friends about how awful my mother is. I mean, she forgot her own child *again*.

    b. Call my mom and maybe not so gently remind her that I am *still* waiting to be picked up.

    c. Pray that my mom is okay. She's been pretty stressed out lately, and I know she's doing her best. I shoot her a text to see if she needs me to catch a ride with a friend.

7. My coach cut me from the big game, even after I worked so hard during practice. I can't believe I'm not starting. I:

    a. Quit the team, because I will never be good enough.

b. Stop trying to earn the coach's approval. I'll just do whatever and get through the season.

c. Pray that God will give me the determination and skill I need to be a better player. There are a lot of really great players on the team, and I plan to support my teammates whether or not I play.

8. I have never felt lonelier. Eating lunch by myself is routine now. I don't know why, but slowly my friends ghosted me. I:

a. Think about harming myself. No one sees me anyway.

b. Start eating lunch in the library. I might as well knock out some homework while there are no distractions.

c. Pray that God will meet me in my loneliness and ask him to bring new friends into my life.

If you answered mostly As, you are a Weapon Bearer. There is still some training to do. Flex your spiritual muscles by picking up your Bible, digging into the Word, and looking up passages that encourage you in your current circumstances. As a Weapon Bearer, the enemy has had moderate success in convincing you of his lies—but not for long.

If you answered mostly Bs, you are a Skilled Swordsman. While you are making progress on the battlefield, you still need help controlling your weapon as you defend against the enemy's attacks. Specialized training in the Word of God can help you better prepare for your next battle. In addition to wielding your sword of the Spirit, spend time praying before acting.

If you answered mostly Cs, you are a Bible Ninja. You take time to train, pray, and prepare for battle. When the enemy engages, you are not so quickly knocked off your feet. Remember a good soldier continues to train so that their skills and reflexes stay sharp. Be vigilant and keep up the good work!

The Sword of the Spirit—Then versus Now

A Roman soldier's sword, known as the *macaira*, could be up to two feet long, fashioned by a blacksmith, with a hard carbon coating on the blade and handle, which would have been made from ivory, wood, or bone. Each sword was personal and customized for the soldier who was wielding it. A sword needed to be accessible and ready to use, and a soldier needed to be skilled and proficient with his weapon. Soldiers who didn't practice regularly did not handle their swords well in battle, when these weapons were used in hand-to-hand combat with the enemy.

How does this translate to Scripture? In Ephesians 6:17, when Paul says, "take . . . the sword of the Spirit, which is the word of God (NIV)," he is telling us to pick up our Bibles. The Word of God is the offensive weapon in our spiritual arsenal, and it is a unique revelation of the true and living God. Because the sword of the Spirit reflects our living God, we can use it to cut through every attack and defense the enemy can raise. When wielded by a servant of God, nothing can withstand the sword's ability to cut straight through Satan's deceptions and uncover the truth.

The Bible is called the Living Word because it is God-breathed and timeless. Much like the custom swords crafted for Roman soldiers, God's Word is personalized for each of us. Take a look at the example below:

The passage reads:

> "The Lord your God is in your midst, a mighty one who will save; he will rejoice over you with gladness; he will quiet you by his love; he will exult over you with loud singing." (Zeph. 3:17 ESV)

Now personalize it:

> The Lord my God is in my midst. Lord, I know you are here, and I thank you. You are a mighty King who will save me. You will rejoice over me with gladness. You will quiet me with your love. You will exult over me with loud singing. Thank you, Lord.

Develop the habit and hone your skill at applying God's Word to you personally, as if God is speaking directly to you and through you, because he *is*. When the enemy's attacks are blatantly in your face, draw your sword of the Spirit and cut the enemy down. God's Word will never fail you, and God will never abandon you.

An Effective Weapon

In Matthew 4, Jesus models for us how to effectively wield the sword of the Spirit. We learn from this passage that Jesus was led into the wilderness alone to be tempted by the devil. Jesus fasted for forty days and forty nights, and as you can imagine, he became very hungry. The *tempter* came to Jesus in his vulnerable state and taunted him.

> And the tempter came and said to him, "If you are the Son of God, command these stones to become loaves of bread." (Matt. 4:3 ESV)

Look at how Jesus responds:

> But he answered, "It is written, 'Man shall not live by bread alone, but by every word that comes from the mouth of God.'" (Matt. 4:4 ESV)

And so they went back and forth like this. The devil tempted Jesus, and each time, Jesus responded with Scripture. Finally, Jesus is done when he says, "Be gone, Satan! For it is written, 'You shall worship the Lord your God and him only shall you serve'" (Matt. 4:10 ESV). Guess what? Jesus commanded him, rebuked the devil with Scripture, and Satan had to leave.

Spiritual warfare is scary, no doubt. However, you have the *most* effective offensive weapon for striking back when the enemy attacks. Remember Satan cannot steal your salvation. His mission is to distract, divide, and destroy—pretty much to make the lives of Christians as miserable as possible to keep us from doing the kingdom work God has called us to do.

Luke 10:19 tells us that God has given us authority and power over the enemy:

> Look, I have given you authority over all the power of the enemy, and you can walk among snakes and scorpions and crush them. Nothing will injure you. (NLT)

You have the power to cut Satan and his army down. They may not like it, but when you wield the sword of the Spirit, they *must* obey. So the next time you feel the enemy closing in, take a breath, grab your Bible, and unsheathe your sword. You will be ready for battle. The Lord our God has gone before you (Deut. 31:8), and he will go behind you. You have only to trust, to open your mouth and speak the Word of God, and then watch your enemy flee.

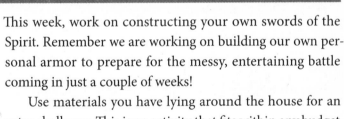

An Activity for Parents and Tweens:
Armor Design—Sword of the Spirit

This week, work on constructing your own swords of the Spirit. Remember we are working on building our own personal armor to prepare for the messy, entertaining battle coming in just a couple of weeks!

Use materials you have lying around the house for an extra challenge. This is an activity that fits within any budget, so be creative and have fun!

This week as you work on your swords, look up passages in the Bible that are meaningful to you. Add these Scriptures to your swords. Visualize tearing and slicing through the enemy's lies to reveal God's truth. Stand firm and know this weapon will not only help you defend against Satan's attacks, but with the sword of the Spirit, you can keep the enemy on the run. When you are finished, pray aloud over your entire armor, using the power of *rhema*. If you are not sure what to pray, try the prayer below.

Dear Father in Heaven,

Bless my sword, Lord, and give me the courage to wield my sword of the Spirit as you have intended. Help me not to leave my sword in its sheath, leaving your powerful Word unspoken, and leaving myself vulnerable to attack. Give me the confidence to accept the assignment you have given me, to step forward on the firm foundation of my faith in your truth. Help me to choose what is right and to lead others who may not know you a little closer to your truth as well.

Thank you for the gift of salvation, Lord. Thank you for loving me so deeply that you sent your Son to save me by grace, to take the punishment for my sins, to free me from the penalty of death. Even when I make mistakes and stray from your flock, you pursue me. You have marked me as your own, and I am so very thankful.

Send your Holy Spirit to reign over my life. Bring to mind just the right Word to be in my heart and upon my lips. Fill me with your Spirit and ready my mind with Scripture to rebuke and push the enemy back. Thank you, Father. I love you.

It is in your Son's name I pray,
Amen.

What's Your
SITREP?

It's time for a situation report, so let's check your understanding and dig deeper into the context of Chapter Seven.

1. Do you think spoken words have power? Discuss why or why not.

2. Based on what you learned this week, write down the definition of *graphe*, *logos*, and *rhema* below. Which power do you wield with the sword of the Spirit?

3. Look up 2 Timothy 3:16–17 and write it in the space below. What does this passage of Scripture mean?

4. What is more powerful when rebuking Satan—reading God's Word silently or reading it aloud? Talk with Mom or Dad about your answer.

5. Look up Hebrews 4:12 and write it in the space below. How powerful is the sword of the Spirit?

6. Have you ever experienced a situation that you knew Satan was responsible for? How did you respond? How did the enemy respond?

7. Read Isaiah 40:8 and write it in the space below. What does this passage say about the longevity of God's Word?

8. Write down three ways you can become more skilled at wielding the sword of the Spirit.

9. Look up and read 2 Timothy 3:16–17. What does it say about which Bible passages are helpful for teaching and personalizing God's message?

THIS WEEK'S **BATTLE PLAN**

1. Talk about your dexterity with the sword of the Spirit. Look at the "Sword of the Spirit Challenge" in the Appendix. Commit to the training plan that will help you become a more accomplished swordsman or swordswoman. Open your Bible and try your hand at personalizing Scripture. *Battle tactic: Becoming intimately familiar with your personal sword of the Spirit will better prepare you to cut through the enemy's deceptions and defense, ensuring you are prepared for battle on both the defensive and offensive fronts.*

2. Continue to pray the armor of God aloud over yourself and each member of your family. Put that *rhema* to work!

Letters from the Battlefield

Dear Friend,

I know what it's like to be lonely. I know what it's like to be surrounded by a large group of people and still feel alone. I am a very extroverted individual who absolutely loves to socialize with others. I am usually energized by spending time with people. However, despite my love for getting to know others, in the core of my spirit, I still feel as if I don't truly know anyone.

In the past few years, Satan has tried to use loneliness to distract me from my faith. Growing up, instead of attending public school like most of my peers, I attended a small private school. When I reached high school, I was less concerned about the social aspect of it and more concerned about making my goal of attending Texas A&M University a reality. (Goal achieved! Whoop!) Because of this goal, my parents and I collectively decided that homeschooling would benefit me better in the long run.

Since switching to unconventional schooling, my circle of friends has morphed into a much smaller and tight-knit community. I went from having a few close friend groups to only having a couple close friends. In traditional schools, teens are offered many opportunities to partake in social events and make friends. Compared to homeschoolers, these individuals have more chances to build lasting friendships through different types of social organizations, school clubs, school sports and teams, and even classes. Unlike my traditionally schooled peers, my circle of friends this year is filled with my family, my "tribe," my church community, and a handful of homeschoolers.

In church a few weeks ago, we discussed community, how it evolves as we change, and where we see God reflected within our communities. We each shared the types of communities we participate in and how each unique community impacts our life. One girl in my small group (for the sake of not mentioning names, I'll call her Susie), who I consider one of my close church friends, spent quite a while explaining all of her various circles of community. Susie is an extrovert who loves to be involved in as many social activities and events as she can, and because of this, she seems to have a ton of friends. While she was sharing, I found myself feeling sad and lonely. I felt as if I was just another person in one of her many circles, which was not the type of friend I consider her to be for me. It took me a few days to realize that I was under Satan's attack. He was using loneliness and my desire for a close community to distract and draw me away from my faith, and it almost worked.

My mom is my best friend. She is someone I can always confide in, so her words usually hold a lot of weight. It was shortly after this tearful recollection that my mom shared an analogy with me that opened my eyes to an important truth. This is when she shared the bus analogy with me. My mom told me to visualize myself on a bus to my God-given destination or my short-term goal (Aggieland). Throughout my ride, I will encounter many individuals. Some will sit with me for a while until their stop arrives and it's time for them to hop off the bus. I may sit by myself for a while before someone else takes a seat. Perhaps there are other people on the bus not sitting with me but headed in the same direction for a bit. There will even be times where the bus driver and I are the only people aboard. However, once I reach my destination, I will see that there are others who were headed to the same place as me but they took different routes.

My mom used this analogy to help me understand that while it may be lonely now, this season is not forever. I am also not alone. That is a lie the enemy whispers in my ear to distract me from the truth. I am not a lone soldier on the spiritual battlefield, despite what the enemy would have me believe.

No one said the spiritual battle would be easy. In fact, the battlefield can be a very daunting place when you feel lonely. When you are feeling alone, it is easy to fall into the enemy's snares and believe you are a solitary soldier on the battlefield with him. However, we need to remember that despite our earthly loneliness, we are never truly alone. God is always with us, and he has given us the most powerful weapon to defend against the enemy. That weapon is the sword of the Spirit, and it will never fail us in battle.

Words have power. As Christians, we know exactly how powerful words can be. Our Heavenly creator literally spoke our universe into being (Gen 1:3). We are crafted in God's image, which means our words have power too (Gen 1:26). My parents instilled in me at a young age the importance of using my voice. My mom and dad taught me the importance of vocalizing my defense against Satan. For as long as I can remember, my family has always collectively rebuked Satan when he attacks. Family is everything to us—a special community that will always love you, stand with you, and defend you. I recognize that not everyone has this experience, and I am thankful for the gift of family that God has given me. I can recall countless times when my family stood together and declared, "Satan, get out of our house! You are not welcome here. We praise only one God, and his name is Jesus."

The Bible teaches us in 2 Timothy 3:16-17, "All Scripture is God-breathed and is useful for teaching, rebuking, correcting, and training in righteousness, so that the servant of God may be thoroughly equipped for every good work" (NIV). By using our God-breathed Scripture and God-given voice, we are wielding the sword of the Spirit. The enemy despises Scripture, and he will always flee when it is spoken. This is why we must not leave words unsaid. Like my mom said, when we choose to stay quiet, we are choosing to leave our sword in its sheath.

Friend, Satan works hard to win each battle and spiritual trial, but God has already won the war. Even so, Satan will not tire in his efforts to distract from the truth. Whether he uses loneliness, anxiety, drugs, sex, or a myriad of other distractions, he cannot steal your salvation in Christ. You are not defenseless, and you are not alone. Stand your ground, use your voice, and slay the enemy with the truth.

Love your friend,
Ashley

Dear Friend,

When I was younger, my parents decided to put me in a small, private Christian school. At times, however, it didn't feel very Christian. In that environment, I wasn't expecting to encounter as many uppity "I know God more than you do" types of people. It made me feel <u>less than</u>. I was not welcomed by other girls in my class, and sometimes they even spread rumors about me to new-comers, encouraging them not to speak to me because I was focused on trying to be a good student and would not conform to who they thought I should be. I didn't like nail polish, and I wasn't obsessed with boys.

So what? Is this how Christians are supposed to act? Was there something wrong with me? All these questions ran through my head over and over whenever I sat by myself through many lunches. A voice would whisper in my ear, "If this is how Christians are, why should you be Christian? Why don't you just cave and be like them? What's wrong with you?" When I caved to these lies, I would freeze up and fall into a pit of self-pity and depression that was nearly impossible to climb out of.

The Lord, however, kept me safe. I felt very close to him during this time. The Lord was my friend. I talked to him during lunch, and he kept me from knowing true loneliness. I was never without the Lord walking beside me, the Holy Spirit countering the whispers of the enemy. Instead of the sting of the enemy's lies, I heard, "You are mine. I love you. I have chosen you, so don't worry about them. Nothing is wrong with you." However, I was and still am very much in the spiritual battle.

I have to decide if I'm going to listen to Satan's lies or lean on God's Word and his truth. Discerning the truth from the constant noise inside your head is so tough, but with God, nothing is impossible. Fighting back with the sword of the Spirit against the lies is the only way to cut through the enemy's relentless pushing toward the pit of self-pity and depression. Even then, I can only do this with the help of my King. We must fight back. We must always fight back.

When I was in the depths of my depression, the hardest thing to do was to ask for his help. I felt like a failure. Why should the Lord of All, who created the whole world, help me? But then he would whisper to me, "Because I love you. I sent my Son to die on the cross for you." That's the ultimate truth, ladies and gentlemen. God loves us. Grasping that truth, I would then pray for help. The enemy would love to keep us in his pit of lies and self-pity, but God has better plans for you and me than sitting in the muck. He wants to free us from the grip of the enemy, to free us from that awful, stifling pit so we can breathe fresh air!

Friends, remember that you are loved by the Creator of the Universe. How cool is that?! Satan's lies may plague you, yes, but when you hear them, and you feel yourself inching toward the pit of despair, pray and remember how God has armed you with a potent and powerful weapon. He has armed you with his truth and the ability to use that truth to defend against the enemy's schemes and attacks.

The Lord is good, y'all. He is so, so amazing, and he loves you. <u>You</u>! No matter what you've done or what lies you have believed, your worth is given to you by God—not by your friends, not by fame, not by wealth, not by anything this world has to offer. When someone asks me who I am, no matter what I've done, I say I am a Child of the One True King. You are, too. Stand up! Pick up your sword and fight against the lies of the enemy with the powerful Word of God. You are made for so much more than the enemy tells you. You are royalty!

In him,
Paige

NOTE

[1]Catherine Bird, *The Art of Amen* (Abilene, TX: Leafwood Publishers, 2019), 136–37.

PART THREE

A Winning Strategy

Pray in the Spirit at all times and on every occasion.
Stay alert and be persistent in your prayers
for all believers everywhere.

Ephesians 6:18 (NLT)

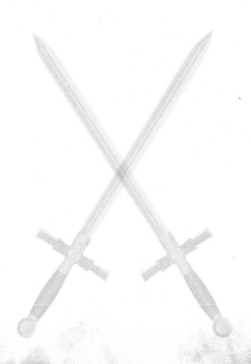

Chapter Eight

Understanding Prayer

*The earnest prayer of a righteous person
has great power and produces wonderful results.*

James 5:16 (NLT)

Why Prayer?

Paul says in Ephesians 6:18, "Pray in the Spirit at all times and on every occasion. Stay alert and be persistent in your prayers for all believers everywhere" (NLT). Before we unpack Paul's instruction further and talk about the how and why of prayer, let's discuss what prayer *is*. Simply stated, prayer is an open, honest conversation with God. The first time we see prayer mentioned in Scripture is Genesis 4:26:

> When Seth grew up, he had a son and named him Enosh. At that time people first began to worship the Lord by name. (NLT)

However, if we define prayer as simply an open, honest conversation with God, then the first prayers actually began in the Garden of Eden with Adam and Eve, who openly enjoyed fellowship with God before the first sin. Prayer enables us to have a relationship with God, which is further deepened through the Word of God. Healthy relationships consist of speaking *and* listening, so it stands to reason our prayer life with God should reflect both. As we pray, our relationship with God grows.

A Model for Prayer

The best example we have for prayer was modeled by Jesus himself. Look at the following passages where the Bible shows that Jesus prayed:

> Then Jesus went with them to a place called Gethsemane, and he said to his disciples, "Sit here, while I go over there and pray." (Matt. 26:36 ESV)

> One day soon afterward Jesus went up on a mountain to pray, and he prayed to God all night. (Luke 6:12 NLT)

> Jesus repeatedly left the crowds, though, stealing away into the wilderness to pray. (Luke 5:16 *The Voice*)

Scripture provides evidence that Jesus prayed, and he prayed often. Through God's Word, we learn *how* Jesus prayed as well. We often see Jesus praying *with other people*. Look up Luke 9:28 and write it in the space below.

Luke 9:28

This passage tells us that Jesus took some of his disciples into the mountain with him to pray. Through passages like this one, Jesus demonstrated the importance of praying together.

Jesus prayed *for others*. Scripture shares examples of Jesus's intercessory prayers—prayers for other people. Read Luke 22:32 and write it in the following space.

Luke 22:32

Jesus also prayed *alone*. I love that while Jesus taught us the value of praying together, he also modeled the importance of praying alone. Look back at Matthew 26:36 and write it in the space below.

Matthew 26:36

Scripture makes it clear that prayer was very important to Jesus. He demonstrated to us that prayer is purposeful and effective. The Bible tells us Jesus rose early in the morning, sometimes went without sleep, and withdrew in solitude—all for the sake of prayer. Through prayer, he made decisions, performed miracles, and overcame difficult situations. In contrast, we often only pray when we have time. Jesus showed us prayer was an integral and seamless part of his human life. His prayer reflected his personal relationship with God, and he trusted in God's will regardless of the outcome of his earnest requests.[1]

We aren't Jesus, so we will certainly fall short of the model of prayer he gave us. However, God doesn't expect you to be anyone or anything other than the authentic person he created you to be, and that is the person with whom he longs to have a relationship. Only I can share my heart with God, because there is only one me. Only you can share with God from the depths of your heart, because there is only one you. In the words of the wise Dr. Seuss, "Today you are You, that is truer than true. There is no one alive who is Youer than You."[2]

An Effective Battle Strategy

Paul understood that prayer has an important role in the spiritual battle around us, which is why Ephesians 6:18 is so significant. He includes prayer as part of the spiritual armor of God, not as an afterthought or a new idea. Paul intended the armor of God to be put on *with* prayer.

While praying in solitude is important and we should carve out alone time with God regularly, prayer does not necessarily mean stopping what you are doing and secluding yourself from the world. Be encouraged to embrace prayer as a natural act of worship that fits seamlessly in your day-to-day life.

And yes, the enemy will try to distract you, because that's what he does. Those distractions come in many forms—the phone rings, a Snapchat or text pops up, your dog needs to go outside, your mind wanders—the list is endless. I find that when distractions are rampant, I am usually on to something important. This means the enemy is threatened by whatever I am praying. When this happens to you, unsheathe your sword of the Spirit, rebuke the enemy, and soldier on!

A Framework for Prayer

Think about when you are in a room full of people and someone is asked to pray. How many people jump at the chance to pray aloud in a crowd? Probably very few. The truth is many of us feel a little nervous when offering a prayer in front of others. While public speaking can be daunting for sure, some of us even may be uncomfortable praying alone.

We can be comforted that we are not the first to struggle with prayer. Even the disciples were unsure about how to pray. Thankfully, Jesus provides a framework for how we should pray in the Gospel of Luke. In the following passage of Scripture, Jesus taught us the Lord's Prayer:

> One day Jesus was praying in a certain place. When he finished, one of his disciples said to him, "Lord, teach us to pray, just as John taught his disciples."
>
> He said to them, "When you pray, say:
> 'Father,
> hallowed be your name,
> your kingdom come.
> Give us each day our daily bread.
> Forgive us our sins,
>   for we also forgive everyone who sins against us.
> And lead us not into temptation.'" (Luke 11:1–4 NIV)

The Lord's Prayer is more than a framework for prayer, though. It's also a framework for a relationship with Jesus. If prayer is an open, honest conversation with God, the Lord's Prayer provides a solid foundation for us to build on. Take a few minutes to think about how you can personalize the Lord's Prayer, and write your thoughts in the space below.

Father

hallowed be your name

your kingdom come

Give us each day our daily bread

Forgive us our sins

for we also forgive everyone who sins against us

And lead us not into temptation

Remember why personalizing Scripture is so important in the spiritual battle against Satan and his dark forces. The Bible is God's living Word, and we know it is the most potent offensive weapon we have against the enemy. Combining Scripture with our prayers is *powerful* and *effective*. Hone your skills as a Bible Ninja so you will be prepared when the enemy launches his next attack!

G-R-A-C-E
A Prayer Tool

There are a lot of different prayer tools we can use during our quiet time. The following is a tool my parents and tween teams have used for years in Bible study. It is simply another way to guide you through prayer time if you have a little trouble getting started. Take some time this week to try this prayer tool, and perhaps try your hand with a few others as well!

G-R-A-C-E

Gratitude   Begin and end your prayers by thanking God.

Repent   Confess your sins and ask for God's forgiveness.

Ask   Lay your requests at God's feet, for he tells us to come boldly before him.

Consider   Listen and reflect on what God may be saying back to you.

Esteem   End your prayer with praise and worship for a God who loves you more than you could ever possibly imagine.

God is *relational*. He wants to spend time with you. Don't overthink your prayers. Just be you and share your heart. That is all God expects of you!

The Helper

Think about the many types of prayers we pray. Sometimes our prayers are whispered in public, with our families, in the closet, in the shower, in the car, in the classroom, during a Zoom meeting, in our hearts without our voices, and the list goes on. Sometimes we pray as one person, and sometimes we pray as many. Sometimes we have words, and sometimes we don't. What happens in those moments when life circumstances feel so heavy and hard that we just can't think of the words to pray?

It is in these instances when the Holy Spirit, also called the Helper (John 14:26), speaks for us; he intercedes on our behalf.

> A similar thing happens when we pray. We are weak and do not know how to pray, so the Spirit steps in and articulates prayers for us with groaning too profound for words. Don't you know that He who pursues and explores the human heart intimately knows the Spirit's mind because He pleads to God for His saints to align their lives with the will of God? (Rom. 8:26–27 *The Voice*)

The Holy Spirit entered you when you made the choice to give your life to Christ and become a Christian. Scripture tells us the Holy Spirit's purpose is to help us in our walk of faith. The Holy Spirit is just as present as the Father and the Son, even though it may be tougher to wrap our heads around the idea of him.

There are many aspects to the Holy Spirit's personality, one of which is to intercede on our behalf. In those instances when you honestly cannot think of a single word to pray, bow your head, close your eyes, and trust the Holy Spirit to pray to God on your behalf.

God Always Responds

Do you ever wonder if God answer prayers? He absolutely does. Always. He answers *yes*, *no*, and *not yet*. God's timing is also often different than ours. I don't know about you, but in the middle of a test when you have forgotten an answer to a question and pray for God to help you, most likely you're hoping God's response is going to be pretty immediate. That's not always the case, though.

My mom was diagnosed with stage IV cancer four years ago. No matter how old you grow, there is never a time when you're ready to lose your mom. She was a steadfast presence in my life, and I talked with her every day, often more than once. News of her diagnosis was devastating.

She fought the awful disease valiantly for nearly nine months as my family prayed and prayed and prayed that God would heal her. And he did heal her. God just didn't heal her as we prayed he would. We wanted God to heal her earthly body, but God wanted to heal her completely. She stepped from her hospice bed into the arms of Jesus, and now my mom feels no more pain.

More recently, my husband changed jobs rather unexpectedly, as I mentioned in an earlier chapter. He worked with his old firm for nearly fifteen years, so he wanted to ensure a smooth transition for the team he was leaving behind. His replacement was hired but unable to start for three months, so his soon-to-be former boss asked if he could continue working his old job while working his new job at the same time. It wasn't ideal, but he decided to give it his best, and it was *rough*.

It became clear rather quickly that he could not sustain the schedule and pace he was keeping, so we prayed that God would provide a way for him to transition completely much sooner than we had anticipated. Then, one afternoon, my husband received a call from the guy who was planning to take his position at the old firm. The man had been let go from his employer unexpectedly and needed to start his new job (my husband's old position) as soon as possible. This meant my husband would be transitioning within a couple of weeks instead of a few months. Woohoo! While we didn't rejoice that this poor man had lost his job, we did rejoice that God had provided a quick response to our prayer. God did not answer our prayer in the way we thought he would, but he provided for us nonetheless.

Our God is a God of love, and he is also deeply personal. God is holy and wise, and he knows what's best for us. No one understood this better than Jesus. While he was on earth, Jesus modeled for us how we should talk with God by praying to God himself. On the night Jesus was betrayed and arrested, he prayed to his Father, asking for a reprieve from the torture and death he knew awaited him.

> And going a little farther he fell on his face and prayed, saying, "My Father, if it be possible, let this cup pass from me; nevertheless, not as I will, but as you will." (Matt. 26:39 ESV)

Look how Jesus ended his prayer. Even though he dreaded what was to come, he concluded his prayer with a statement of complete obedience to God—"not as I will, but as you will." Is this how you pray? When you pray, are you committed to God's will or your own? Regardless of whether God says *yes*, *no*, or *not yet*, his answers are always, *always* intended for our good.

One Last Reminder

Well done, soldier! We have unpacked your spiritual armor, explained the landscape of the battlefield, and taken a closer look at the enemy. You are battle ready! As we wrap up our study on the armor of God, remember:

- Jesus has already secured victory, which he did when he died on the cross for our sins. Our enemies have already been defeated by means of the cross (Col. 2:15).
- Nothing can separate us from the love of Jesus—*ever* (Rom. 8:38–39).
- As followers of Jesus, we have been given power over the enemy (Luke 10:19).
- We should pray without ceasing on all occasions (1 Thess. 5:17).

When the seas are raging in those stormy seasons of life, it can be especially difficult to trust God's perfect timing. Sometimes I can sense God moving in the present, but often I see him best when I look back at all he's done around me. This week's activity invites you to work in your prayer journals. Take some time to research other people who recorded their prayers (like George Müller). You might be surprised once God calms the storms and crashing waves just how abundantly clear his presence remains, even though you had trouble hearing that small whisper in the howling winds. God is our constant in all seasons and circumstances of life.

> Trust in the LORD with all your heart
> and lean not on your own understanding;
> in all your ways submit to him,
> and he will make your paths straight. (Prov. 3:5–6 NIV)

An Activity for Parents and Tweens:
Prayer Journals—Yes, Even Boys Use Prayer Journals!

Wrap up any last adjustments on your armor. You'll need to be battle ready this week!

Also, take some time this week to make a new prayer journal. Be as creative or as simple as you like. The goal is for deeper, more meaningful fellowship with God. Your prayer journal is simply one tool you can use. Some folks may prefer a simple notebook, which is just fine! Use what works for you.

Inside your prayer journal, though, be sure to date your prayers. Then leave room to go back and write down how God answered each one. Use the GRACE acronym to help you with the framework for your prayers, or use another prayer acronym that works for you. There are plenty of options to choose from. The important thing is that you are praying regularly, so try not to get tripped up in the format of your prayers. God cares what you have to say, and he loves any method you'll use to talk with him.

Remember God's timing is different than ours. Some prayers will be answered quickly, while others may take a little longer. God always answers prayers—whether it's *no*, *yes*, or *not yet*. Look up Jeremiah 29:11 and write it in the space below.

Jeremiah 29:11

God's answers are always intended for our good, so trust in his wisdom, even when he answers a prayer in a way you don't quite understand. You are precious and worthy in God's eyes, and your time with him will always be time well spent.

Go forth, prayer warriors!

What's Your
SITREP?

It's time for a situation report, so let's check your understanding and dig deeper into the context of Chapter Eight.

1. Where does prayer fall on your list of priorities? Is it a have-to or a want-to?

2. What types of distractions do you encounter when you pray?

3. Look up Matthew 18:20. Why is it important to pray *with* other believers?

4. What do we call prayers for other people? Read John 17 and write down who Jesus prayed for and what he prayed for them.

5. Is it easier to pray when things are going well or when things are falling apart? Why do you think that is?

6. Read Romans 8:26–27. How does the Holy Spirit help us when we pray?

7. When we pray, are we committing to God's will or our own?

8. Look up Matthew 26:41 and write it below. What does "the spirit is willing, but the flesh is weak" mean?

9. Read 1 Kings 19:11–13. Do you pray hoping to hear or see a visible response from God? What can we learn from Elijah in this passage?

10. What things in your life might make it difficult for you to hear God's whisper?

THIS WEEK'S **BATTLE PLAN**

1. Spend time in prayer as Jesus modeled for us: praying with others, praying for others, and praying alone. Think about the distractions Satan uses to interrupt your prayer time with God. Each day this week, make a conscious effort to pray throughout your day. *Battle tactic: The more we practice, the more naturally our prayers will come. The enemy has less chance of distracting you when prayer is seamlessly integrated into your day.*

2. Continue to pray the armor of God aloud over yourself and each member of your family. Thank God for the relationship you have and ask him to reveal himself to you in new ways with each coming day. Focus on deepening your friendship with Jesus as you would with a new pal from school or church.

Letters from the Battlefield

Dear Friend,

When I was younger, I started my prayers to God with, "Dear God. Hey, I'm sorry that I'm bothering you . . . but . . . ." Then, I would talk to him about whatever would be on my mind at the moment and end with, "I'm sorry, I won't bother you again." I never knew what to pray about, felt worried about whether my prayers were significant or not, and wondered if I was even worthy of talking to him.

I worried about not communicating with God correctly because I wanted to please him and do, correctly, one of the few things our Lord asks, which is to have a relationship with him. In his song "Watching You," Rodney Atkins says, "He closed his little eyes, folded his little hands, and spoke to God like he was talking to a friend." This lyric helped me realize what I had to do. It did not require some long, beautiful prayer that everyone would love. I had to express my feelings, tell God about my day, and reflect on my life. We develop our relationship with God by talking to him. As with any other relationship, to build trust and grow, we must communicate regularly.

My designated time for prayer is before I go to bed. I keep my lamp on so I won't fall asleep and tell God about my day, its highs and lows. I also pray in the hallways at school or while I am in my car. I don't kneel and fold my hands. Instead, I silently pray something as simple as how thankful I am for raindrops on my windshield. I have noticed that I pray just as much, regardless of whether good or bad things are happening. God wants all of us and every part of us. Sometimes I have trouble telling him about my friends or school. However, silence works as well. God already knows what is in our hearts and minds.

I did not always find it easy to pray, especially while I was awaiting confirmation. Eighth grade was difficult—most of my teachers were unforgiving, I had severe knee surgery, and my wisdom teeth had to be removed. During that time, I could not find the motivation to talk to God. I didn't want to face the consequences of my actions, and admitting the sins that I had committed to God just made them more real. Three months later, I actually went through confirmation of my faith and earned membership in my church. During confirmation, I knelt in front of my congregation, family, and minister. To say I was nervous about even bending my knee is an understatement. But when I did kneel, it felt like a warm, weighted blanket was wrapped around me. I physically felt a weight on me, and I knew that the weight I felt was God. At that moment, I knew that God was aware of everything I had been feeling over the past six months—that he had felt those emotions with me. I knew that while confessing my sins and burdens is a good thing, in that moment, I did not have to. My Father already knew and had forgiven me.

After ninth grade, I decided I wanted to change high schools. The private Christian school I was currently attending was awful, and I could not emotionally handle being there anymore. I felt this was because everyone acted as if they were superior. For example, in one incident, my coach wanted me to coach the JV volleyball team. He told me that if I wanted to keep playing volleyball at the school at all, I would have to coach the JV team, not be on the JV team, or there would be no team at all. It was too much pressure, and I felt emotionally drained beyond what was healthy. Thankfully, I was able to transfer schools over the span of three days. I knew the decision I had to make would impact my life for years to come. It was a family decision, but fortunately the final verdict was based on what I wanted and, more importantly, what I needed. My parents gave their input, but they would not make the decision for me. I depended on God to guide me. I made a list of pros and cons and discussed the situation with my best friend for hours. What helped me most during this time was praying to God or, like it says in this book, "stepping into battle." I learned through prayer that if I wanted to pour more of myself into my relationship with God and other people, I would also have to pour into myself—I cannot fill up someone else's cup if mine is empty.

Since I changed high schools, I've become content, and I am happy. After I changed schools, the realization hit me that I have friends who love me and that I am emotionally healthy and stable; this brings me tears of joy. I am happy because I realized that if I want to share and enjoy my life with friends, I can. Praying to God is important in order to have a relationship with him. Pursuing and communicating with him is the only way for any relationship to work.

Blessings,
Abigail

Dear Friend,

Life is a vicious battlefield where the devil is constantly
on the prowl, looking for a moment where he can grab a
foothold and tear you down. While it may seem grim, God
has provided us a weapon to combat Satan with: prayer.
Prayer is a discussion with God. In the same way that
your relationships with friends grow when you talk to
and hang out with them, when you pray, you grow closer
in your relationship with God. As your relationship with
Christ grows, so will your trust in him.

    After much prayer over what to write, God put it on
my heart to tell you this story so that you may learn
how important prayer is and how a relationship with
Christ can make a huge change in your perception regarding the world and the challenges that the devil will try to
use to dishearten you. Recently, I was in a relationship.
Unfortunately, I began to feel as though the relationship was coming to an end. For weeks, I pleaded with
God, asking him to mend the relationship so we could
stay together. On a Friday night, I decided to flip back
in my prayer journal. (Yes, I have a prayer journal, even
though I'm a guy. They are very useful for keeping you
focused on praying and help keep your mind from wan-
dering; most importantly, you can look back and see a
physical record of the prayers God has answered.) As I
was saying, I was flipping back to my old prayer entries.
Many of them were about growing a closer relationship
with my girlfriend, which led me to plead more with Christ
for my relationship to work out. As I continued to flip

further back, I began to read entries before I was dating, and they said, "Lord, I pray that you will help me to find the woman that you have chosen as my wife. I ask that she loves you unconditionally and that she will strengthen my relationship with you and vice versa." After reading this, a peace that only the Spirit can provide came over me. I then prayed, "Lord, I'm afraid the relationship that I am in is about to end. I hope not, because I still have feelings for her. . . . I ask that if it is possible that we can work it out, but if your ultimate plan is for us to marry someone else, please make it clear. I ask that you will help us work it out, but ultimately let your will be done on earth as it is heaven."

The next day, we met and our relationship ended. While this hurt immensely, I had a sense of peace, knowing that God has the bigger picture in mind and that while I may have pain now, I know God has the right woman out there to be my wife. In addition, it is also comforting to know that God has the best in mind for her as well. The only reason I have this peace is because of my constant prayer over the matter. As I pray to God and merely talk to him about everything I'm grateful for, worried about, or upset over, I have grown closer to him. Due to this closer relationship, I am able to trust that he has what is best for me in store.

I trust God to determine my whole future; he knows what's best for me. This kind of trust can only exist in a close relationship. As I said earlier, the only way to create a close, trusting relationship with God is through prayer. Prayer doesn't have to follow strict rules or guidelines. If you struggle to pray, the GRACE acronym is a helpful tool for getting you started. Now, I don't know the details of the relationship you have with your father, but every evening, my father will ask me how my day was and then prompt me to tell him what I did that day. Just as my earthly father wants to know about what I have done every day, our Heavenly Father wants you to tell him everything about you. Charles Crozat Converse and William Bolcom said it best in their song "What a Friend We Have in Jesus":

What a friend we have in Jesus
All our sins and griefs to bear
What a privilege to carry
Everything to God in prayer . . .
Can we find a friend so faithful
Who will all our sorrows share?
Jesus knows our every weakness
Take it to the Lord in prayer

Pray over everything, and Christ will be with you in everything. He may not answer the way you hope, but it is always for the best. Just trust him. As you strap on each piece of the armor of God, praise God and ask him to grant you wisdom and strength to fulfill his mission. Even though the enemy's focus is mighty, never forget that God is mightier and always with you.

Your Fellow Soldier,
Hayden

NOTES

[1] Bird, *Art of Amen*, 31–33.

[2] Dr. Seuss, *Happy Birthday to You!* (New York: Random House, 1959, 1987).

APPENDIX

FACILITATOR'S GUIDE

A Note to Facilitators

Facilitators, this guide has been prayerfully written to aid you in small group study. Your primary role as a small group leader is facilitating discussion at your meetings. For some, this opportunity is exciting and thrilling. For others, the task feels daunting. Regardless of your comfort level with leading small group study, my goal was to write a guide that would make facilitating a less intimidating task. Within the pages of this guide are discussion questions and small group activities to help parents and tweens unpack Scriptures more fully, digging deeper into the heart of the study.

At your first meeting, I recommend asking your group members (parents and tweens) to sign a covenant of confidentiality (see the "Sample Bible Study Covenant" included in this Appendix). This particular study is about understanding and actively using our individual armor of God. Some discussions may prompt group members to be vulnerable and share deep personal insights. In order to foster a transparent discussion about the sensitive topics included in this study, all group members should feel safe to share. It is important to discuss this in your first meeting as you stress confidentiality within your small group. Your small group covenants are also a great tool for confirming participants' commitment of time and attendance.

Format of the Study

This study is unique in that it is not broken down by daily reading and study. While the study itself can be completed in eight weeks, this guide is a nine-week-long class designed to facilitate joint Bible study and discussion between parents and their tweens. Each week, we will examine a topic related to the armor of God and add layers to these discussions as parents and tweens dig deeper into the study. The study is full of relevant Scripture passages and conversation starters to get parents and kids thinking and talking about how these excerpts from God's Word are still relevant for us today.

Walk through the nine-week plan and briefly touch on the topics of study. Again, technically, there are eight weeks of study with a week of introduction to the topic of spiritual warfare. This can be easily consolidated or adjusted to fit another timeline, so parents and tweens should feel empowered to approach weekly study however it fits into their schedules. If they want to read a little bit each day, great! If it works better for them to consolidate everything into two days, excellent. This study is intentionally flexible.

Each week, parents and kids will also have an optional activity related to the armor of God. Encourage class participants to do these activities if at all possible, as they relate to each week's theme and will be just plain fun! These weekly activities are age appropriate, fun, and a different approach from traditional study, to help parents and their kids discuss, connect, and learn about Scripture together. Also, the relevance of the armor of God in our lives as Christians leads naturally to a discussion of struggles that individuals may be currently experiencing.

Walking through this study with my daughters, I realized my own children were facing spiritual battles that I had no idea were raging. The intention for this study and my prayer for every participant is that they strip the enemy of his power by breaking down his lies, reinforcing God's Word and the truth that we are all deeply and unconditionally loved. It is an opportunity to be intentional about spending time as parent and tween, drawing closer to one another while deepening our individual relationships with God. I pray the time spent digging into Scripture results in an affirmation that the battles you and yours may be facing are *temporary* and that the war has already been won.

WEEK ONE

Open each class time with prayer. During your first meeting, take the first ten to fifteen minutes to make introductions. Pick one of the following icebreakers (or use one of your own) so parents and tweens are able to get better acquainted.

The M&M (Mix & Meet) Icebreaker

You will need a bag of regular chocolate M&Ms. Be sure to tell your participants not to eat them! Assign a different meaning to each color candy. For example:

Blue = Family
Green = School
Yellow = Friends
Red = Hobbies
Brown = Music/movies

Set a limit to the number of candies each person can take (usually five to ten, depending on your group size). The number of M&Ms each person has in their hands is how many facts they will share with the group. For example, if one person has four red candies and one brown, they would share four facts about their hobbies and one fact about their favorite music or movie.

Toilet Paper Game

Take a roll of toilet paper and ask each person how many squares they want, but don't tell them what they are for. Set a limit from five to ten. Count out the number of requested squares, and give them to each class attendee. Repeat until all the participants have the requested amount of toilet paper squares. After everyone has taken their tissue, ask each parent and tween to share something about themselves for every square of toilet paper they have taken.

Human Rock-Paper-Scissors Game

Decide as a group which full-body pose will signify each element (i.e., rock, paper, scissors). After the poses are decided, break participants into pairs. Have pairs face each other and count down from three (i.e., three . . . two . . . one . . . SHOOT). On "SHOOT," each person will strike one of the three poses. Rock beats scissors, scissors beat paper, and paper beats rock. You can play as many rounds as time permits. The best out of five rounds is the winner. Or have fun and change up partners! Another variation: Take the "winner" of each round, pairing winners together until the final two battle for the title of Ultimate Human Rock-Paper-Scissors Champion.

God and the Family Bond

Give each parent and tween a list of questions you have made up ahead of time. Use your imagination to make a list of twenty or more preferential questions, like "Who is your favorite movie star?" or "What is your favorite book?" You can ask about colors, music, plays, TV shows, or hopes for the future. Place two columns next to each of the questions—one for the parent and one for the tween. Ask each parent and child to write down their own favorite and what they think is their parent's or kid's favorite. The pair then goes over the list together. Take a few minutes to talk about how God knows us better even than our own family.

Human Treasure Hunt

Create a list of fifteen to thirty statements to distribute to the parents and kids in your small group. Give the group a period of time to find people who meet the different criteria of the different statements on the list. When participants find someone who meets the criteria, they ask that person to sign their list. At the end of the activity, read off the various statements and ask anyone who meets the criteria to stand up. A sample list may include:

- Has a blue toothbrush
- Is an only child
- Hates chocolate
- Is having a very happy *un*birthday today
- Can stand on her head and count to ten
- Has two sisters
- Has brown eyes
- Had a shower yesterday

Getting Started with *The Armor of God*

After your class participants have had an opportunity to greet one another, it is a good time to ask parents and tweens to take out their Bibles. Discuss different Bible translations and the benefits of referencing different versions throughout the Bible study. If a passage is difficult to understand in one translation, encourage the participants to try another.

Ask someone to read Ephesians 6:10–13. Take a few minutes so others can share from different Bible translations they may be using. (It may be helpful for the facilitator to bring two or three different translations to class.) The purpose of this exercise is twofold:

- It demonstrates a helpful strategy during Bible study when a passage is difficult to understand: check another translation!
- Ephesians 6:10–13 is a great passage to begin *The Armor of God* with. This study is about understanding and unpacking the armor of God, as explained by Paul to the Ephesians. The first chapter discusses the landscape of the spiritual battlefield.

Preparing for Chapter One

The Armor of God Bible study is about the spiritual armor God has given us to withstand Satan's attacks. Part One of the study is foundational, providing the landscape for the spiritual battle that wages on the earth between believers and an unseen enemy. In the first chapter, readers learn about the unseen spiritual war and the enemy who attempts to sneak into our camp like a lion in the night. Who is the enemy, and how can we recognize him when he attacks? How can we prepare for and defend against his attacks? We are going to talk about all these questions and more over the course of this Bible study.

The first week is about understanding that the spiritual war is a battle we cannot see. Even though we may not be able to see the spiritual war raging around us, it is indeed happening. Take a few minutes to reread Ephesians 6:11–12 again, and ask parents and tweens to share what they think Paul means.

What Is the Unseen War?

Listen to their responses, and try to gently include any quiet group members who may not be participating in the discussion.

Tug-of-Spiritual War

Materials Needed:

- Rope (20 feet or more, depending on the size of your group)
- Yardstick

Separate your group into two teams—perhaps parents against tweens. However you split your group, make sure there is the same number of people on each team. Ask your teams to grab either side of the rope, and place the yardstick in the middle as the line of demarcation. For those who have never played tug-of-war, explain the rules of the game.

Tell participants the rope represents our spiritual life, and each team represents either good or evil. Play several rounds, change up teams, and have fun!

Afterward, come back together as a group and discuss:

- Satan is relentless as he works to distract and divide us from God. However, God works even harder to draw us closer to him and remind of us of who we are and whose we are.
- The spiritual battlefield is like a tug-of-war as Satan tries to convince us of his power and influence, but he has already been defeated.
- Talk to participants about how the enemy can make our lives pretty miserable, but he does not control us. (When we accept Jesus into our hearts and ask him to be our Lord and Savior, we are marked as Christ's own. Satan knows this and is powerless to separate us from God.)
- Ask if there is anyone who has not asked Jesus into their hearts and if they might like to say that prayer tonight.

Thanksgivings and Prayer Requests

Take the last ten minutes or so of each small group time to share thanksgivings and prayer requests. Give thanks to God for creating each and every one of us with love and detail. Ask God to give us the wisdom and truth to see ourselves and others as he sees us.

These young men and women are prayer warriors in training, so keep them in the habit of praying for others and giving thanks when God answers prayers—even if he doesn't answer them the way we thought he would! If resources permit, think of including small notebooks for your class participants, so they may take notes and jot down prayer requests during each meeting. Providing simple notebooks and supplies for participants might be a crowd pleaser for boys and girls alike. Poll your participants and decide what's best for your small group.

Blessings to you, facilitators! You are planting important seeds of faith. Thank you.

WEEK TWO

Open the class time with prayer. After prayer, welcome everyone and take the first few minutes of class for each person to share one blessing they experienced since the last time you were together as a group.

Follow-Up from Chapter One

Allow some time for parent/tween teams to share their thoughts and experiences from Chapter One. Here are some potential questions for discussion:

- Ask group members to remind you about the unseen war. What is it?
- Do you believe spiritual warfare is real and happening around us every day?
- In the unseen war, who is fighting? Which side are we on?
- Why do you think Paul used the analogy of a Roman soldier?
- How is the armor of God relevant for Christians today?
- Ask tweens to look up and read James 4:7. If time permits, allow them to share from different Bible translations. Talk about the enemy's response when we use God's Word to rebuke him. Take a few minutes to talk about how this makes participants feel.
- Did anyone relate to the "Letters from the Battlefield"? How did your group respond to Abby's and Breck's letters? Did they prompt any additional discussions at home?

- Has anyone started the Parents and Tweens Armor of God Activity? Are there any initial thoughts and impressions? Take time to discuss what your end-of-study battle may look like. Will you use colored powders? Or messy substances?

The Belt of Truth

After answering any questions about Chapter One, direct the discussion to the topic for Chapter Two. The next chapter is about the belt of truth and its purpose. The belt of truth is arguably the most important piece of the armor of God. Centrally worn around the waist, the Roman soldier's belt was more functional than even today's most bodacious fanny pack. This week, tweens and parents will learn the essential function the belt played in "girding one's loins" and holding the other pieces of armor together. Together as a small group, you will explore the difference between truth and deception and why God's truth is so foundational to defending against Satan's schemes.

Two Truths and a Lie Game

Assemble group participants into a circle. Each person prepares to share three statements: two truths and one lie. In any order, each person takes a turn sharing the three statements with the entire group. The object of the game is to figure out which statement is a lie. The rest of the group votes on each statement, and then the person reveals which one is the lie.

Gird Your Loins

This is a fun demonstration of how to "gird" one's loins!

This activity is adapted from http://www.artofmanliness.com/articles /how-to-gird-up-your-loins-an-illustrated-guide/.

Materials Needed:

- An old sheet (× however many teams you plan to have)
- Scissors (to cut head and armholes in the sheets)

Cut and prepare the sheets ahead of time.

Divide your small group into teams (either parent/tween or parents against tweens). Follow the steps below and give your teams a couple of minutes to practice. Then set a timer (the recommended time is two minutes) and challenge your teams to be the fastest in the girding of loins!

1. First, fashion your sheet into a tunic by using the scissors to create holes for your head and arms. Then, put on your tunic and hoist it up so that all the fabric is above your knees. This will give you mobility.
2. Gather all the extra material in front of you, so that the back of the tunic is snug against your backside.
3. Once the excess fabric is gathered in front, pull it underneath and between your legs to your rear. This should feel kind of like a diaper.
4. Gather half the material in each hand, bringing it back around to the front.
5. Finally, tie your two handfuls of material together, and you'll be all set for battle!

Junk-in-the-Trunk Game

The object of this game is to be the first to empty the "junk in the trunk."

Materials Needed:

- Kleenex box (qty. 4)
- Belt (qty. 4)
- Duct tape
- 32 ping-pong balls

Empty the Kleenexes and remove the plastic window from each box. Cut slits on each side of the box, large enough to slip a canvas belt through. Reinforce the corners with duct tape.

Each player should strap on a belt and box, taking care to ensure the box is resting just above their backside. Place all eight ping-pong balls in the box. You should have enough for four participants to compete at the same time. Set your timer for one minute and explain that once the timer begins, each person should jump, wiggle, and shake until all eight balls are out of the box. They will have one minute to complete their task! Play a few rounds as time permits.

True or False Bible Game

Explain to your small group that you are going to play a game that shows the importance of knowing what the Bible says. For each "true" statement, participants will stand up. For each "false" statement, participants will squat to the ground.

The group leader then calls out the following:

1. Mary was Jesus's mother. (T)
2. Zacchaeus built the ark. (F)
3. Moses roasted marshmallows at the burning bush. (F)
4. Jacob killed Goliath. (F)
5. Malachi is the last book of the Old Testament. (T)
6. Jonah was swallowed by a catfish. (F)
7. Cain killed his sister Mabel. (F)
8. Five loaves and two fish were used to feed five thousand people. (T)
9. There are twenty-seven books in the New Testament. (T)
10. The slave traders took Joseph to Babylon. (F)
11. Paul was a missionary. (T)
12. Jacob had no children. (F)
13. The prodigal son was hired to work as a house painter. (F)
14. Jesus died on the cross. (T)
15. Jesus thought children should stay back while he was teaching. (F)
16. Jesus prayed in the Garden of Gethsemane. (T)
17. Chick-Fil-A was served at the Last Supper. (F)
18. Mark was the first Christian martyr. (F)
19. Barnabas went with Paul on some of his mission trips. (T)
20. Bananas are a fruit of the spirit. (F)

Ask group members how easy it was to pick out the false statements. Ask what they can do to increase their ability to recognize the truth. *Hint:* Read the Bible more often! Challenge your participants to read their Bibles every day so they can increase their knowledge of the truth.

Thanksgivings and Prayer Requests

Take the last ten minutes or so of the class to share thanksgivings and prayer requests. These young boys and girls are prayer warriors in training, so keep them in the habit of praying for others and giving thanks when God answers prayers—even if he doesn't answer them the way we thought he would!

WEEK THREE

Open the class time with prayer. After prayer, welcome everyone and take the first few minutes of class for each person to share one blessing they experienced since the last time you were together as a group.

Follow-Up from Chapter Two

Allow some time for parent/tween teams to share their thoughts and experiences from Chapter Two. Here are some potential questions for discussion:

- How do you know when something is true?
- Is there such a thing as absolute truth—something that is true at all times in all places? (Note: This is a good opportunity to talk about the infallible Word of God and why God's Word is the standard by which we measure truth.)
- Look up John 17:15–17 and read it aloud as a group. What does Jesus pray? What does it mean to be set apart by the truth?
- What is the purpose of the belt of truth?
- Take a few minutes to talk about personalizing Scripture. Ask the group if they think this is important. Why or why not? Lead them in a discussion about how God's Word is timeless, always relevant, and most definitely personal. When we personalize God's Word, we are impressing it further into our hearts, which takes away any foothold for Satan to plant his lies and deception.
- Did anyone relate to the "Letters from the Battlefield"? How did the group respond to Jacob's and Madi's letters? Did they prompt any additional discussions at home?

- How are the armor designs coming along at home? If you haven't yet, begin talking about a date/time for your final *battle*. It should be a fun celebration after the conclusion of this study.

The Breastplate of Righteousness

After answering any questions about Chapter Two, direct the discussion to the topic for Chapter Three. In this chapter, parents and tweens will further unpack Ephesians 6:12 as they learn about the breastplate of righteousness, which defends the heart and guides us in choices of *right* living. The breastplate of righteousness comes after the belt of truth, because in order to know what is *right*, one must know what is *true*. Tweens and parents will walk through how God calls us to live as Christians and subsequently why the enemy works so hard to deceive us into making poor choices—choices that do not honor God. In this chapter, readers also discuss why we should be aware of the enemy but not afraid of him. We are to keep our focus on the ways of the Word while the enemy works to keep our focus on the ways of the world.

Special note: This week's activity is especially messy, so be sure to give your small group a heads-up prior to your meeting that they will need a change of clothes. Prep them so that they come appropriately attired in clothes they don't mind getting stained.

"Right Living"—A Messy, Fun Lesson

This activity is adapted from http://www.BetterBibleTeachers.com.

Materials Needed:

- Twister game
- Blue liquid dishwashing soap
- Mustard
- Ketchup
- Relish (squeezable bottle works best)
- Disposable garbage bags or a drop cloth

Preparation: Cut garbage bags to lay open and flat or use a large disposable garbage bag or drop cloth. This protected area should be a little larger than the Twister mat. Set up the Twister game on top of the garbage bags or drop cloth.

Invite your small group to remove their socks and shoes and ask them to sit around the perimeter of the game area. Explain to your group that you're going to play a game of Twister. For those who have not played the game before, explain the rules. Tell participants that Twister really tests the limits of our flexibility and balance.

Take a minute to admire the cleanliness of the Twister board. Let group members know the Twister board is representative of our hearts. Each circle represents a unique quality that makes each of us who we are. Explain that God has crafted each of us with love and purpose. God wants us to love him, to learn about him, and to help others come to know him. Satan tries hard to distract us from our purpose and the truth of who we are by tempting us into sin. These are called *spiritual attacks*.

Next, ask for a volunteer. Give them the ketchup bottle. Share a possible scenario: Your friend shared a secret with you, but you thought it was no big deal and actually kind of entertaining. You shared your friend's secret harmlessly with a few other friends, thinking they would also find it funny, which they did. Now everyone at school is talking about the thing that your friend shared privately with you, and your friend is humiliated. You broke your friend's trust and spread gossip, even though you didn't mean for it to backfire so badly. You've messed up. You've sinned, and now your heart is a little messy.

Ask your volunteer to squirt ketchup in the red circles on the Twister mat.

Ask for another volunteer. (Hand them the mustard.)

Explain the next scenario: Your mom told you twenty more minutes of electronics and then it was homework time. Mom gets distracted and you manage another hour of game time before she pops her head back into your room. When she asks if you've completed your homework, you lie and say yes, because you just want to complete one more level. You can always finish your homework later, but you don't and end up copying a friend's homework quickly before class the next day. That's also sin, and that makes your heart a little messier.

(Instruct the volunteer to pour the mustard over the yellow circles.)

Ask for another volunteer. (Hand them the relish.)

Next scenario: Let's say your friend gets a new phone, and it is so cool. And you really, really, really want a new phone, not your parent's hand-me-down. You keep thinking about that phone, dreaming about that phone. Suddenly, your phone doesn't seem good enough. You're no longer thankful that you even have a phone at all. You can only think about your friend's phone and how much better your life would be if you had that phone. You start coveting that phone. That also makes your heart a little messier.

(Have your volunteer put the relish on the green circles.)

Ask for another volunteer. (Hand them the blue dishwashing soap.)

Another scenario: At practice, the same annoying bully starts calling you names . . . again. Of course, your coach doesn't hear. Instead of taking it, you push back and start calling the bully really awful names—but nothing he doesn't deserve. You know he only lives with his mom and start listing all the reasons why his dad probably left them. Finally, the bully leaves you alone, but it came at a pretty high price. That's also sin. Even though it's not sin that you committed first, it's still a sin, and it still makes your heart messy.

(Ask your volunteer to pour the blue soap on the blue circles.)

Ask: When our life is messy with sin, how easy is it to stay upright and keep our balance?

Take time to play a couple of games of Twister. Let parents and kids play as long as time permits. Afterward, give participants a chance to change their clothes and clean up. Come back together as a group a discuss:

Was it tougher or easier to stay up when you had all that mess on your feet? It was undoubtedly way tougher. Explain this is what it's like when Satan tempts us with sin. When we make a choice that doesn't honor God and who he has called us to be, life feels harder. The more we sin, the tougher it can be to do the right, clean thing. When we give in to the temptation to sin, it can make a mess in all areas of our lives. Stepping in the ketchup, the mustard, the relish, or the soap gives us a pretty messy demonstration of what sin can do to our lives. It can get pretty slippery and messy, which may cause us to fall down, and sometimes we take others down with us.

God wants us to have clean hearts, not messy ones. He wants us to do what is called *right* living, which means we strive to live righteously. We can't do that on our own, though. Everyone sins. No one is perfect, which is why the gift of salvation through our belief in Jesus Christ is such good news!

When we confess our sins, we ask God to wash away the mess of sin and clean our hearts. (Dump water onto the Twister board and clean away the mess.) Once our hearts are clean again, we should try our best to make choices in life that honor God—saying *yes* to righteousness and *no* to the temptation of sin.

Wise Choice

This game shows how temptation and sin are often wrapped in an appealing package, but once we get past the appealing outer layer, the bitter and awful-tasting truth of sin becomes apparent!

Materials Needed:

- BeanBoozled Jelly Belly Game (enough for your small group to try at least two rounds)

Thanksgivings and Prayer Requests

Take the last ten minutes or so of the class to share thanksgivings and prayer requests. Encourage group participants to write down prayer requests each week in their own prayer journal or notebook. These young boys and girls are prayer warriors in training, so keep them in the habit of praying for others and giving thanks when God answers prayers—even if he doesn't answer them the way we thought he would!

WEEK FOUR

Open the class time with prayer. After prayer, welcome everyone and take the first few minutes of class for each person to share one blessing they experienced since the last time you were together as a group.

Follow-Up from Chapter Three

Allow some time for parent/tween teams to share their thoughts and experiences from Chapter Three. Here are some potential questions for discussion:

- What is righteousness or right living?
- What is sin? (*Any word, thought, or action that falls short of God's will.*)
- Read Romans 3:23 together. Give group participants who have different Bible translations a chance to share. What does this passage say about all people?
- What is the purpose of the breastplate of righteousness?
- Why does it come after the belt of truth? (*In order to know what is right, we must know what is true.*)
- Where does righteousness come from? Can it be earned?
- Why is it important to guard our hearts? Ask participants to sing the old song "O, Be Careful Little Eyes What You See." Is there truth to these lyrics?
- Discuss situations or areas in our lives where we might struggle to make the *right* choice. What about the gray areas? Talk as a group about what gray areas look like and how we can determine *right* choices when faced with uncertain circumstances.
- Discuss ways we might seek *right* living as Christians.
- Did anyone relate to the "Letters from the Battlefield"? How did the group respond to Baylee's letter? Did this prompt any additional discussions at home?
- Spend a few minutes addressing any questions about the armor designs at home. How is each team doing on their designs and constructions?

The Sandals of Peace

It's time to turn the group's attention to Chapter Four. Satan comes like a thief in the night to steal our shoes and rob us of peace. Although the enemy cannot steal our salvation, he can attempt to make our lives pretty miserable. This comes in the form of life events that leave us disoriented, disappointed, and distracted—a divorce, a bad grade, a horrible fight with a friend, and so forth. This is a tried and true tactic the enemy uses to knock us off balance. However, the sandals of peace help us recognize these types of spiritual attacks. A closer look at Shadrach, Meshach, and Abednego reveals that while God does not always change our circumstances, he most certainly meets us in the middle of whatever "fire" we may be facing. In this chapter, tweens and parents will also discuss the importance of holding tight to the peace that surpasses all understanding as they are sharing the gospel with others and the importance of building community with other believers.

Walk-the-Line Game

Run a line of masking tape along the floor, eight to ten feet in length.

Materials Needed:

- Colored masking tape
- A variety of shoes: heels, boots, rain boots, etc. (You can ask group participants to help with this.)

Ask parents and tweens to walk the line of tape in their own shoes. Then, have them take off their shoes and try to walk the line again in another pair of shoes. They should have a difficult time walking the second time.

Explain how Paul used the analogy of a Roman soldier, because their shoes would have fit perfectly. They would not have been able to engage in battle with shoes that were slippery or kept them off balance. They needed shoes that kept them firmly grounded and ready for whatever enemy came their way. Likewise, our spiritual armor must be outfitted with appropriate footwear. Our shoes must be fitted with the gospel of peace.

The *gospel of peace* means the good news of peace that Jesus brings. Take a moment to look up John 16:33 and ask participants to take turns reading aloud from their Bible translations.

Examples:

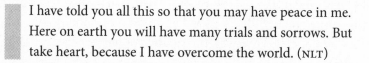

> I have told you all this so that you may have peace in me. Here on earth you will have many trials and sorrows. But take heart, because I have overcome the world. (NLT)

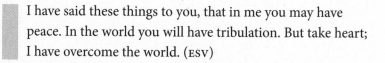

> I have said these things to you, that in me you may have peace. In the world you will have tribulation. But take heart; I have overcome the world. (ESV)

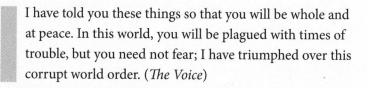

> I have told you these things so that you will be whole and at peace. In this world, you will be plagued with times of trouble, but you need not fear; I have triumphed over this corrupt world order. (*The Voice*)

Just as Roman soldiers were sent on a mission, so were the disciples. Guess what? We are, too! Take the next few minutes to read Matthew 28:16–20, and talk about the Great Commission. Remind group participants about when this takes place (after Jesus has risen from the dead and spent time with his disciples). Talk about what this means for Christians today.

Slip 'N Slide Race

Remind group participants ahead of time that they will need socks for your meeting this week. For this game, you will need slippery floors (not carpeted). Run a line of masking tape at either end of the room, like a goal line.

Materials Needed:

- Blindfolds (enough for one blindfold per pair—as many pairs as your group wishes)
- Masking tape

Ask participants to take off their shoes and set them to the side. Divide your small group into two teams (perhaps parents and tweens for the first round and then mix it up), and then line the teams up on opposite sides of the room. Give each team blindfolds. Each team should pick one person to be a "guide." Their job will be to lead their blindfolded teammates to their team goal line, which will be made clear by the small group leader. Each team should be on the opposite end of the room from their own team goal line. With the guide's hands on one of their teammate's shoulders, it is the guide's job to get their teammate to the goal line quickly and safely.

All team members that are not playing the role of the guide or the blindfolded person can distract the opposing team's pair. When the small group leader calls "time," the object is for team members to hinder their *opponents'* path to their respective goal line. Be creative! Your teams may even set up obstacle courses. Small group leaders, use discretion to ensure the safety of your group members.

Give team members a chance to switch up players. Play a few rounds. Come back together and discuss how difficult it was for the blindfolded teams to fight against an enemy they couldn't see. Explain how the shoes of the gospel of peace *and* our guide (the Holy Spirit) help us stand firm, even through the ups and downs of life. When we have Jesus as our savior, we receive *his* peace, a peace which surpasses all understanding. What an important piece of our spiritual armor!

Shoe Soup

Before everyone puts their shoes back on their feet, toss all the shoes into a pile on one side of the room. Have participants stand on the other side of the room. Once everyone is in place, ask them to run to the pile of shoes and grab a pair that is not their own. They need to find the person whose shoes they have and help that friend put their shoes on. Tell them they must take turns and cannot put their own shoes on their feet. Everyone should work together to ensure the entire group has their shoes on correctly before coming together in a circle at the end of the game.

Just like in the Christian race, we are not designed to run the race alone, only looking out for ourselves. Once everyone has their own shoes back on their own feet, discuss as a group why community is important for Christians as we strive to live out the Great Commission.

Thanksgivings and Prayer Requests

Take the last ten minutes or so of the class to share thanksgivings and prayer requests. Group members should write their prayer requests down in whatever way works for them. Encourage them to go back as you discuss and share how God is answering their prayers. These young boys and girls are prayer warriors in training, so keep them in the habit of praying for others and giving thanks when God answers prayers—even if he doesn't answer them the way we thought he would!

WEEK FIVE

Open the class time with prayer. After prayer, welcome everyone and take the first few minutes of class for each person to share one blessing they experienced since the last time you were together as a group.

Follow-Up from Chapter Four

Allow some time for parent/tween teams to share their thoughts and experiences from Chapter Four. Here are some potential questions for discussion:

- What does the gospel mean? (*It means "good news." The gospel books in the Bible are Matthew, Mark, Luke, and John, and each one talks about the good news of Jesus.*)
- Is there such a thing as absolute truth—something that is true at all times in all places? (*This is a good opportunity to talk about the infallible Word of God and why God's Word is the standard by which we measure truth.*)
- Take another look at Daniel 3 and the story of Shadrach, Meshach, and Abednego as a group. Does God abandon us to our circumstances? How does this Bible story show us that God can meet us in the middle of our own furnaces of trouble?
- Can anyone share an example of how God has met them in their furnace of fire?

- What is the purpose of the sandals of peace?
- How is the peace of the world different than the peace of Jesus?
- How does Satan attempt to steal our peace?
- What can we do when the enemy tries to steal peace away from us?
- How can we help one another?
- Did anyone relate to the "Letters from the Battlefield"? How did the group respond to EK's and Ethan's letters? Did they prompt any additional discussions at home?

The Shield of Faith

In Chapter 5, tweens and parents delve into what it means to live by faith so that we may take up the shield of faith and thwart the enemy's attempts to plant seeds of doubt in our hearts. Similar to the interactive exercises in previous chapters, the activity in this chapter helps readers become more familiar with biblical examples of those who have shown us how to live by faith despite uncertain and often dangerous circumstances. Tweens and parents also discover more about the relational aspect of God's character and how one of the most effective ways to defend against Satan's fiery darts of doubt is by spending time and deepening our relationship with our Creator.

Blindfolded Trust (a twist from last week's game!)
Pair tweens with their parents for this exercise.

Materials Needed:

- Blindfolds (enough for each team to have one)
- Chairs

Set up an obstacle course in the room using chairs set sporadically throughout the path. Explain that each tween will be blindfolded and will have to listen carefully for the voice of the Holy Spirit (played by their parents for this game) to pass from one side of the room safely to the other. The enemy (played by the facilitator) will whisper false instructions and try to distract each person from their path. Facilitators, you'll be working your way around the room, whispering into the ears of tweens. If their parent whispers instructions to navigate them around an obstacle, try to steer them off course.

Parents should blindfold their tween. When the facilitator gives the word, each tween should turn around three times. Parents cannot touch them. They can only whisper and guide them from one side of the room to the other. Play a few rounds and then discuss how difficult it was to stay focused on the voice of the Holy Spirit with the additional whispers and so many other distractions. How does this translate to how we should listen for the Holy Spirit in our daily lives?

Fiery Nerf Darts

Materials Needed:

- Poster board (enough for every participant to have one)
- Markers
- Paper (8.5 × 11 printer paper is fine, but the sheets will need to be cut small enough so that they can be rolled and stuck into the end of a Nerf dart)
- Scissors
- Nerf guns
- Nerf darts

Cut strips of paper into small squares or strips and ask group participants to write down temptations or situations that Satan might use to make us doubt our faith. Brainstorm as a group (divorce, horrible fight with a friend, loneliness, etc.). Once everyone has had a chance to fill out a few papers, instruct your group to roll the papers up and slip them into the ends of the Nerf darts.

Set the darts aside and distribute the poster board and markers. These poster boards are going to be their shield of faith! Ask group participants to decorate their shields however they'd like. Once everyone is finished, it is time to load the Nerf guns and test those shields of faith! Take turns, giving each person a chance to stand behind their shields to see if they can withstand an assault from the enemy's darts of doubt! Afterward, discuss as a group why our faith serves as the first line of defense against Satan's flaming arrows. How effective is each person's shield of faith?

Cotton Wars

Materials Needed:

- Cotton balls (a couple packages)
- Disposable straws (enough for every group member to have at least one)
- Masking tape

Place two lines of masking tape parallel to one another about two feet apart, running lengthwise across the room. Divide your group into two teams (parents against tweens works well, but change it up). Each team stands on the side of the tape closest to the wall, so no one should be standing in the two feet between the two lines. Hand out straws and cotton balls to each team.

The object of the game is to land as many cotton arrows across the enemy's line as possible. If a person hits an opposing team member, they earn three points. Sending one cotton ball across the enemy's line but not hitting an opponent earns one point. The facilitator will have to keep a close eye on the scoring once the cotton arrows start flying!

Instruct group participants to load their straws with their first cotton arrow and then give the word for battle to commence. Cotton arrows *must* be lobbed with air through a straw—so no using arms to lobby them across the lines! The team with the most points wins!

Remind participants why we take up the shield of faith. When Satan and his dark forces shoot arrows into our camp, fiery arrows will be deflected and snuffed out with our shields!

Thanksgivings and Prayer Requests

Take the last ten minutes or so of the class to share thanksgivings and prayer requests. These young boys and girls are prayer warriors in training, so keep them in the habit of praying for others and giving thanks when God answers prayers—even if he doesn't answer them the way we thought he would!

WEEK SIX

Open the class time with prayer. After prayer, welcome everyone and take the first few minutes of class for each person to share one blessing they experienced since the last time you were together as a group.

Follow-Up from Chapter Five

Allow some time for parent/tween teams to share their thoughts and experiences from Chapter Five. Here are some potential questions for discussion:

- What does it mean to have faith? Give group participants a chance to discuss what this looks like outside of church. For example, Dylan tells Hailey he will take notes for her at school. What does it mean if we say Hailey has faith that Dylan will take notes as he promised?
- Talk about the difference between faith and positive thinking. (*Faith means being able to rely on someone to do what they promised to do.*)
- Ask your group members to look up and read Hebrews 11:1 aloud. Give those who have different translations a chance to share. What does it mean to have "confidence in what we hope for?"
- How does our society and culture confuse faith with positive thinking?
- Do you trust and believe in God's Word? Give group participants an opportunity to discuss why or why not. (*This is also a good time to remind members of their small group covenant and confidentiality.*)
- Sometimes people say one thing and then do something else entirely. Ask your group to respond honestly. Is the risk to follow Jesus in today's culture worth it when Christians are viewed so negatively?
- Are Christians held to a higher standard? (*Yes.*) Ask your small group to look up and read Matthew 7:13–14 aloud. Talk as a group about what this means.

- Faith leads to action, and God often uses our circumstances to reach others who may not know him. Is this an encouraging or scary thought? Give participants a chance to share.
- What kind of flaming arrows does the enemy use against you? If you had to name the flaming arrows, what would they be? (*Anxiety, anger, sadness, distraction, etc.*)
- Did anyone relate to the "Letters from the Battlefield"? How did the group respond to Victoria's and Emily's letters? Did they prompt any additional discussions at home?
- Take a few minutes to address any questions about the process of making their armor. Is anyone having trouble? Do they need help?

The Helmet of Salvation

Much like the helmet of a Roman soldier would have protected his brain and head, the helmet of salvation gives our minds protection from Satan's schemes. In Chapter Six, tweens and parents will explore what salvation means and unpack biblical context to better understand the blood price Jesus paid to cancel our debt of sin. Once we accept the free gift of salvation, our perspective is changed. Readers will also walk through the stark contrast of our spiritual characteristics before and after we accept salvation and what is expected of believers once their eyes have been opened to the truth. We accept the calling to know Christ and to make him known, but sharing the good news in today's culture can be an overwhelming task. Through biblical examples and tools, tweens and parents will glean insight on how to express and share their own salvation story with others.

Musical Hats

Materials Needed:

- A variety of hats (bicycle, ball cap, chef, sombrero, cowboy, etc.) (*Ask participants to bring hats for this game. There should be one hat for each participant.*)
- Music (*Use your phone or another small speaker.*)

Send a reminder prior to today's meeting for each parent and tween to bring a hat. Each player for this game will need their own hat. For example, if Shay is bringing her son and daughter to the small group gathering, she'll need to bring three hats. Small group leaders, you may want to be prepared with a few extra hats just in case some of your participants forget.

Give every group participant one hat to wear. Explain that when the music begins to play everyone will toss their hat into the circle and dance. The facilitator should fish one hat out of the circle while the participants are dancing. When the facilitator stops the music, everyone should quickly grab a *different* hat than the one they had before and place it on their head. The person without a hat at the end of the free-for-all is out. Continue playing until you have a winner!

When you come back together, discuss the purpose of hats. What benefits do they provide? (*They protect our eyes from the sun, identify a team we play on, keep our heads warm, etc.*) Let your group brainstorm. Then ask in what way the helmet of salvation is like a hat. (*It protects our thoughts/mind.*)

Look up 1 Thessalonians 5:8–11 as a group and take turns sharing from different Bible translations. Talk about how the helmet of salvation protects our minds against bad thoughts, despair, discouragement, doubts, and so on.

Temptation Knock-Out

Materials Needed:

- Plastic cups (a sleeve of Solo cups or something similar)
- Ping-pong balls (15–20)
- Masking tape
- Sharpies
- Small candy pieces for prizes (such as Starbursts or Hershey's Kisses)

Before you begin, pass out the cups and Sharpies and ask group participants to write a word on their cup that represents a way Satan attacks our faith. Some might write *depression*, *anxiety*, self-doubt, and so on.

Brainstorm as a group and then write the words on the cups. Set up five plastic cups on a ledge. If there's space, set up three groups of cups so that three people can play at once. Mark the player's line about ten to fifteen feet away from the cups with a strip of masking tape on the floor.

Give each player five to seven ping-pong balls and tell them that the object of the game is to knock out the devil's temptation. Players should attempt to knock the cups off the ledge using the balls. Let each group participant take a turn. (*Facilitators, make sure you have enough cups for every person to play at least one round.*) Pass out candy for every cup that is knocked off the ledge.

Cheesy Puff Throw

This activity is adapted from https://www.ministryark.com/lesson /helmet-salvation-childrens-lesson/.

Materials Needed:

- Disposable shower caps (one for each participant)
- Shaving cream
- Cheesy puffs (enough bags for each person to use a handful—and then some leftover for snack!)

Divide your group into teams by parent and tween. Distribute shower caps to each person. Between each two-person team, decide who is going to be *it* first. The *it* person will put on the shower cap. Their teammate will put a healthy serving of shaving cream on top of the shower cap. Then, when the facilitator says *go*, the *it* person for each team will try to outrun their teammate. While the *it* person is running, the other team member is chasing after the *it* person, throwing cheesy puffs. The goal is to get as many cheesy puffs as possible stuck on the top of the shower cap. The person who lands the most cheesy puffs wins! After the first round, have team members switch places and play again.

After the game, reassemble as a group. Talk about how the enemy works really hard to impact our mind and land as many *hits* as possible, knocking us out of the spiritual battle. However, with our helmets of salvation, we can defend against Satan's attacks and protect our minds!

Thanksgivings and Prayer Requests

Take the last ten minutes or so of the class to share thanksgivings and prayer requests. These young boys and girls are prayer warriors in training, so keep them in the habit of praying for others and giving thanks when God answers prayers—even if he doesn't answer them the way we thought he would!

WEEK SEVEN

Open the class time with prayer. After prayer, welcome everyone and take the first few minutes of class for each person to share one blessing they experienced since the last time you were together as a group.

Follow-Up from Chapter Six

Allow some time for parent/tween teams to share their thoughts and experiences from Chapter Six. Here are some potential questions for discussion:

- Why do you think the helmet of salvation is a helmet instead of a shoe or a sash?
- What does it mean to be saved, and what are we saved from?
- Read Matthew 22:35–38. What does it mean to love the Lord with your mind? Now read Romans 8:5–11. Talk as a group about how it is different to live by the ways of the world (the ways the flesh desires) versus the ways of the Word (the ways the Spirit desires).
- Ask your group to describe the world before Jesus came. Why do we need a Savior?
- By now, you have built trust as a group. Ask if everyone has invited Jesus into their hearts. Is there anyone that has not prayed the prayer of salvation and would like to do so today? (*This can be a really special moment and an opportunity to welcome a new member to God's family. Take time to pray if a group member asks, and then celebrate accordingly!*)
- When we talk about sharing our testimony, what do we mean? What is a testimony, and why is it important to living out the

Great Commission? (*This is a good time to revisit what the Great Commission is; see Matt. 28:16–20.*)

- What obstacles do we face when sharing our testimony? Give your small group a few minutes to share and encourage one another.
- If you were the only face of Jesus to someone who did not know him, what would they see by spending time with you? Does knowing you make them want to know Jesus better?
- Did anyone relate to the "Letters from the Battlefield"? How did your group respond to Andrew's and Juju's letters? Did they prompt any additional discussions at home?
- How are those pieces of armor coming along at home? Is everyone preparing for the final battle?

The Sword of the Spirit

Tweens and parents have already learned about their protective armor of God, so now we turn their attention to their only offensive weapon: the sword of the Spirit. Much like previous chapters, readers will glean an understanding of how each piece of armor was used by Roman soldiers and compare how this translates to the armor of God. They learn the difference between *graphe*, *logos*, and *rhema*, and that it is *rhema* they embrace as they wield the sword of the Spirit. A fun interactive quiz provides additional insight regarding readers' swordsman or swordswoman skill level, along with activities they may pursue to help them increase their dexterity with the Word. Lastly, tweens and parents explore the twofold purpose of the sword of the Spirit and why they need not fear when they engage in close combat with the enemy.

Cutting through the Lies

Materials Needed:

- Straight pins
- Markers
- Balloons (deflated)
- Small strips of paper

Pass out strips of paper and markers to group participants. Ask them to write down what they know as God's truth. They can write Bible verses, reaffirming words, and more. Let them brainstorm. After they are finished, pass out the deflated balloons. Instruct participants to roll up their strips of paper and tuck them inside the balloon. Then ask them to blow up the balloons and tie them off. On the outside of the balloons, ask participants to write down Satan's lies: *You are unworthy. You are unloved. No one sees you. God could never forgive you for that. Stealing is fun and totally fine as long as you don't get caught.* Let them brainstorm and write down as much as they'd like.

Explain how the sword of the Spirit allows us to cut through the enemy's lies to God's truth and that we can keep the enemy on the run by saying God's Word aloud. Give them the straight pins, which represent their swords of truth, and allow them to pop balloons and "cut" their way through Satan's lies.

Sword-less Fight

Materials Needed:

- Foam swords (qty. 2)

Cut down one sword so only the handle is left. During small group, ask for two volunteers. Do not give them an explanation. Just give one volunteer the fully functional sword and the other volunteer the sword that has been cut down. They will inevitably ask what to do with the "broken" sword. Explain that they are going to duel. Give them a few minutes to battle. If a couple more volunteers want to try, play a few more rounds as time allows.

Afterward, bring your group back together. Explain why the sword that was cut down (which probably did not fare well in the battles) represents what it's like when we enter the spiritual battlefield without the Word of God. This is why spending time in our Bibles and knowing God's Word is critical to our proficiency with the sword of the Spirit. Ask group members to share some of their favorite verses off the top of their heads. Then, brainstorm scenarios where they might need to wield their own swords of the Spirit. They might talk about fighting with friends, getting grounded for lying, failing a test at school, and more. How might we use the Bible in those situations? Which verses might we find helpful? How can we use God's Word to overcome hopelessness, depression, anger, and so on?

Draw-Your-Sword Race

This activity is adapted from http://www.looktohimandberadiant. com/2013/07/armor-of-god-draw-your-sword-game.html.

Materials Needed:

- Plastic knives
- Sharpie
- Container for the knives (like a coffee can or tall Tupperware)
- Candy for prizes

Prior to your meeting, take the plastic knives and write a variety of Bible verses on the end (just the book of the Bible, chapter, and verse) with a Sharpie marker. For example, at the end of one knife, you might write *1 Corinthians 1:18*. Go back through the Bible passages used throughout the *Armor of God* as a guide, and feel free to add additional verses based on your small group discussions.

During your small group meeting, place the plastic knives with Bible verses in the coffee can or another container. When the facilitator says "Go," each group member will grab one knife, then rush to their Bible to find the verse written on the knife. The first person to locate their Scripture wins the round. Play several rounds as time allows. Then come back together as a group and talk about the importance of being skilled Bible Ninjas and how you can all be better prepared when the enemy attacks.

Thanksgivings and Prayer Requests

Take the last ten minutes or so of the class to share thanksgivings and prayer requests. These young boys and girls are prayer warriors in training, so keep them in the habit of praying for others and giving thanks when God answers prayers—even if he doesn't answer them the way we thought he would!

WEEK EIGHT

Open the class time with prayer. After prayer, welcome everyone and take the first few minutes of class for each person to share one blessing they experienced since the last time you were together as a group.

Follow-Up from Chapter Seven

Allow some time for parent/tween teams to share their thoughts and experiences from Chapter Seven. Here are some potential questions for discussion:

- What is the purpose of the sword of the Spirit?
- What kind of battle do we engage in with the sword of the Spirit? Is it used for offensive or defensive purposes (or both)?
- Look up 2 Timothy 3:16 as a group and take turns reading aloud from different translations. What does this verse say about God's Word?
- How does a person become more skilled at using a weapon?
- How do we practice with God's Word?
- Do spoken words have power? Why or why not? Refer group participants back to Genesis 1:3. What does this passage say about how our world came to be?
- What is more powerful when rebuking Satan—reading God's Word silently or reading it aloud? (*Let your small group answer and then lead them through a discussion about why it's important to speak aloud when rebuking the enemy.*)
- Did anyone relate to the "Letters from the Battlefield"? How did the group respond to Ashley's and Paige's letters? Did they prompt any additional discussions at home?
- Confirm plans for your parent and tween battle in the final week. Is everyone prepared?

The Power of Prayer

Chapter Eight of the *Armor of God* explains the importance and power of prayer. In the introduction to this week's final topic, talk with parents and tweens about practical tips for incorporating prayer into our daily lives. Prayer is how we communicate with God, the Creator of all things. Our God is *relational* and desires a deep connection with all his children. Prayer enables us to have a relationship with God, which is then only further enriched through Scripture. Chapter Eight explores why we pray, examples of prayer modeled by Jesus himself, and a prayer tool (GRACE) that can aid us in our own prayer times.

Post-It Prayers

Materials Needed:

- Post-It Notes
- Pencils or pens

Pass out the Post-Its and ask group participants to write down a few important prayer requests on each one. When they are finished, help them place the Post-Its on their shoulders. As a group, take turns laying your hands on one another's shoulders and praying over them. Talk about the importance of praying, praying *aloud*, and praying as a community.

Prayer Puzzle

Materials Needed:

- Notecards (any size)
- Masking tape
- Chairs or buckets
- Pens and pencils
- Candy for prizes

Before your meeting, break the Lord's Prayer (Matt. 6:9–13) into ten phrases and write one phrase on each notecard. You will need two complete sets of cards for this game. Before your small group arrives, set two separate zones where you will hide the cards. Use masking tape to divide the room if it's easier.

Divide your small group into two groups. When the facilitator says *go*, each team will send one person to find the first card on their side of the room. You can tape cards to walls, on light switches, or underneath chairs. Be creative, but don't make it too difficult for teams to find the notecards! When the first team member finds the first card, they'll need to run back to the starting line and tag the next team member. Then it will be the next team member's turn to find the next card, and so on. Each team is working to find all ten cards and then sort them in the correct order of Matthew 6:9–13. Tell them to use their Bibles if they need help. The first team to finish collecting cards and correctly assemble the verse wins.

Take time after the game to talk about the framework for prayer that Jesus gave us. Brainstorm as a group how they might personalize each phrase of the prayer. This will come in handy as they work through the last chapter of the study!

Prayer Practice

This game includes three separate stations for group members to work through.

Materials Needed:

- Marshmallows (jumbo size)
- Chopsticks (at least two sets)
- Bowls (qty. 2)
- Ping-pong balls (reuse from an earlier week)
- Buckets (qty. 2)
- Sports ball (like a small, soft basketball; qty. 2)
- Portable basketball hoop (kid's version)

You will need three stations, and each station will be set up for two people to play at once. At the first station, dump the marshmallows into one bowl. Place the chopsticks by the bowl, and set the second empty bowl at least a few feet away. The object of station one is to move all the marshmallows from one bowl to the other using only the chopsticks. The marshmallow may *only* touch the chopsticks, and the chopsticks cannot be used to pierce the marshmallows. They have to be moved carefully.

For the second station, place masking tape as the throw line. Set the buckets several feet away from the masking tape line. Instruct participants that they will use the ping-pong balls to make a basket. Each person should strive for ten balls in the bucket.

For the third station, set up the basketball hoop. This time, move the masking tape throw line farther away. Instruct participants to shoot their ball into the hoop as many times as possible in the time provided for each station (which should be two to three minutes).

Divide your small group evenly among the stations, then rotate participants until everyone has had an opportunity to play at each station. Afterward, come back together as a group and discuss how well or not-so-well everyone did at each game. Talk about why practicing would make them better and help them improve their skills. Prayer is very similar. The more we practice, the easier it becomes and the more seamlessly it fits into our day. Brainstorm as a group about how you can practice prayer.

Thanksgivings and Prayer Requests

Take the last ten minutes or so of the class to share thanksgivings and prayer requests. These young boys and girls are prayer warriors in training, so keep them in the habit of praying for others and giving thanks when God answers prayers—even if he doesn't answer them the way we thought he would!

WEEK NINE

Open the class time with prayer. After prayer, welcome everyone and take the first few minutes of class for each person to share one blessing they experienced since the last time you were together as a group.

Follow-Up from Chapter Eight

Allow some time for parent/tween teams to share their thoughts and experiences from Chapter Eight. Here are some potential questions for discussion:

- What *is* prayer?
- Where does prayer fall on your list of to-dos? Is it a *want to* or *have to*?

- What types of distractions do you encounter when you pray?
- Where do you pray? How seamlessly is prayer integrated into your daily life?
- Read Romans 8:26–27 aloud as a group, and give participants a chance to share from different translations. Who is the Helper, and how does he help us when we pray?
- What is the framework of prayer God has given us? What other tools can we use when we feel stumped about how to pray? (*This is an opportunity to go over the GRACE prayer tool and any other prayer tools your group may find helpful.*)
- Did anyone relate to the "Letters from the Battlefield"? How did the group respond to Abigail's and Hayden's letters? Did they prompt any additional discussions at home?

Guess what time it is? It's time to BATTLE!

BATTLE!

This is it, team. This is what you have been training for over the last eight weeks. You are ready to suit up in your spiritual armor and enter the battlefield! By now, hopefully your small group has determined how teams will be formed. The pilot team chose to battle kids against parents, which was so much fun! Do whatever works for your group.

It is highly recommended to battle outside, as you will be messy and clothes will likely become stained. Use colored powders, ketchup, mustard, relish, silly string, or any other messy, fun substance you like.

SPECIAL NOTE: Be sure to take a before and after picture! Then share your group's experience on Instagram and tag @catherinefbird and #armorofGodbattle. Catherine will randomly pick groups from time to time and send them a special surprise, so be sure to post and tag your group photo for a chance to win!

Thanksgivings and Prayer Requests

Be sure to take a few minutes after your celebratory battle to join hands and pray. Give thanks for the opportunity to come together each week, to worship God, and to dive deeper into a relationship with him. Thank him for your people! Those people in your group are part of a God-given community that is designed to make you stronger. Reaffirm your commitment to the Great Commission, keep your battlefield skills sharp with regular use and practice, and go forth in the name of Jesus Christ!

THE SWORD OF THE SPIRIT CHALLENGE

An Eight-Week Training Plan

The following is an eight-week training plan to help condition those spiritual muscles and build dexterity with the sword of the Spirit. Become an expert swordsman or swordswoman by spending time in the Word and training daily!

Each week, work through the verses in the training plan using the following Bible mapping tool. The training plan reflects five days of training in the Word and two days of rest. Try not to cram all your training into one day each week! This type of training is about consistency and adapting a regular habit of investing in God's Word.

You can do this! Your sword has been customized just for you, so let's get started with the Sword of the Spirit Challenge!

Week 1

Day	Bible Verse
Day 1	Genesis 3:1
Day 2	Ephesians 2:10
Day 3	Psalm 8:4–6
Day 4	Revelation 12:7–9
Day 5	Luke 10:19

Week 2

Day	Bible Verse
Day 1	John 8:44
Day 2	John 14:6
Day 3	Colossians 1:17
Day 4	Psalm 145:18
Day 5	Philippians 4:8

Week 3

Day	Bible Verse
Day 1	Romans 1:17
Day 2	John 1:14–15
Day 3	Romans 3:23
Day 4	Romans 6:23
Day 5	Philippians 3:9

Week 4

Day	Bible Verse
Day 1	Colossians 3:15
Day 2	Philippians 4:7
Day 3	Matthew 28:18–20
Day 4	Romans 12:5
Day 5	Ephesians 4:32

Week 5

Day	Bible Verse
Day 1	Hebrews 11:1
Day 2	Matthew 17:20
Day 3	1 Timothy 6:12
Day 4	James 4:8
Day 5	Isaiah 43:1

Week 6

Day	Bible Verse
Day 1	Romans 10:9–10
Day 2	Titus 3:3–7
Day 3	Galatians 5:16–17
Day 4	Romans 12:2
Day 5	Ephesians 1:17

Week 7

Day	Bible Verse
Day 1	2 Timothy 3:16–17
Day 2	Genesis 1:3
Day 3	Psalm 64:3
Day 4	John 15:7
Day 5	Zephaniah 3:17

Week 8

Day	Bible Verse
Day 1	James 5:16
Day 2	Luke 5:16
Day 3	Romans 8:26–27
Day 4	Matthew 26:39
Day 5	1 Thessalonians 5:17

BIBLE MAPPING TEMPLATE

This is meant to be a tool for parents and tweens alike as you invest more time in prayer and God's Word. Try to set aside at least thirty minutes each day. Cut out this page and stick it into your prayer journals! It will be especially helpful if you are embarking on the "Sword of the Spirit Challenge." Note you can download additional templates at http://www.catherinebird.net.

STEP 1—Pray

Begin your quiet time with prayer. Use the GRACE prayer tool if you need a little extra guidance.

Remember, God already knows your heart, but he wants to hear directly from you. As a mom, I can often tell my children's moods by their faces and actions. However, I still want to hear them share with me directly. If you can even fathom, God loves us more deeply than we are even capable of loving one another. He loves us so big and so much. He is not worried about the format of prayer you use. God simply longs for an open, honest conversation with you. You. All you have to do is commit to showing up and opening your heart. Your relationship with God will deepen and grow from there.

G—Gratitude: Begin and end your prayers by thanking God.

R—Repent: Confess your sins and ask for God's forgiveness.

A—Ask: Lay your requests at God's feet, for he tells us to come boldly before him.

C—Consider: Listen and reflect on what God may be saying back to you.

E—Esteem: End your prayer with praise and worship for a God who loves you more than you ever possibly imagine.

STEP 2—Dig into God's Word

Pick a passage of Scripture, and try your hand at Bible mapping! This is another tool to help you become more fluent with the sword of the Spirit. God's Word is timeless, relevant, and personal. Use the following prompts to help you unpack Scripture during your quiet time with God each day.

What are the rules in Bible verse mapping? The first rule in Bible verse mapping is that there are no rules in Bible verse mapping. This is a personal time between you and God, where you set aside time and dig into God's Word, asking him for insight about how the passage applies to you. So here we go!

Pick a Bible verse: _____

Write it down!

Now check a different Bible translation—and write it down again.

Go back and underline key words and phrases that jump out at you.

What is the main idea expressed in this Bible verse?

How does this Bible verse speak to you personally?

Take the Bible verse and personalize it!

SAMPLE BIBLE STUDY COVENANT

Attendance

We commit to arriving on time so as not to disrupt the group process.

The group sessions will begin at 6:30 p.m. and end by 8:00 p.m.

We will begin to gather at 6:15 p.m., but study sessions will begin promptly at 6:30 p.m.

If we cannot attend a class, we will contact one of the facilitators or another class member before the class begins so the class knows we will not be there.

Preparation

We will use the reading and reflections assigned in each lesson as a basis for contributing to the group discussion.

Respect

We will respect one another, accepting what each person shares and not monopolizing time and discussions. We will turn cell phones off or use the vibrate setting if we must have them on for emergencies.

Confidentiality

We will value what is experienced and shared within the group as a treasure entrusted to us for safekeeping. We will not break the confidence entrusted to us by others.

Prayer

We will commit to praying for one another by name.

WORKSHOP APPRENTICE TEMPLATES

For the following templates, you will want to scan them, then enlarge them with the scanner to make sure they are the correct size for you.

TEMPLATE FOR THE BELT OF TRUTH

Using the template below, draw six straps for each soldier with a marker on your cardboard. Each belt will need six straps, so think about how much cardboard or poster board your family may need ahead of time. For example, if you are making three belts, you will need eighteen straps. Use a yard stick or ruler to keep your lines straight. The straps should be long enough to create a loop (for sliding over the belt), so keep that in mind as you are measuring for length.

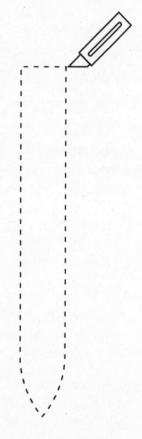

TEMPLATE FOR THE HELMET OF SALVATION

Using the template below, outline the shape of your helmet plume and face mask on poster board. Then use scissors or a box cutter to cut them out.

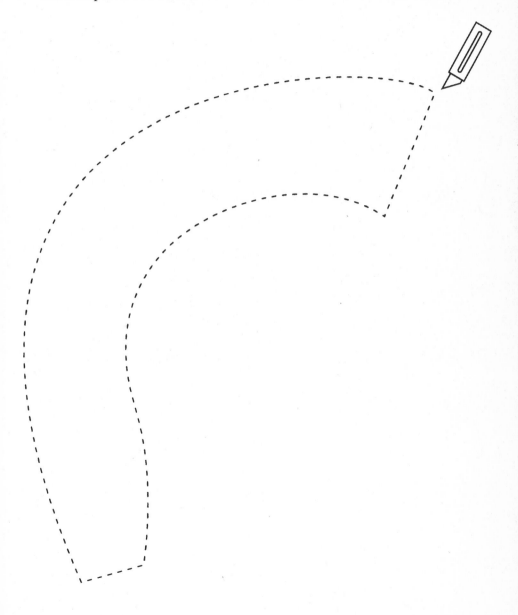

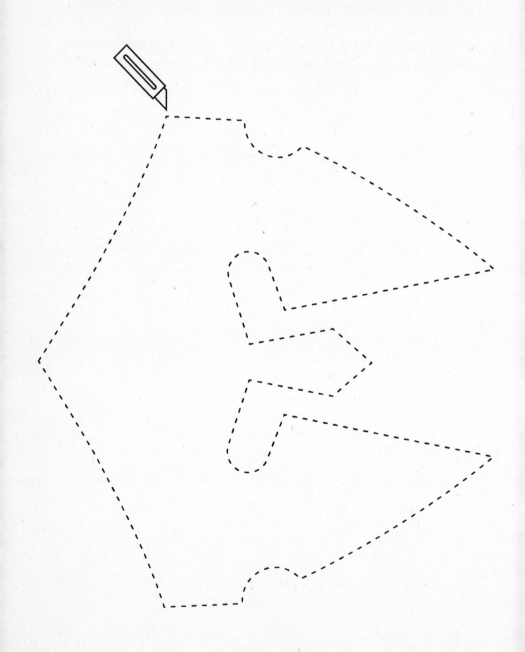

TEMPLATE FOR THE SHIELD OF FAITH

Using the template below, outline the shape of your shield on the cardboard and poster board. Then use scissors or a box cutter to cut the shields out.

Below is the template of a handle for the back of your shield. Trace on poster board two for each shield, then cut them out with scissors.

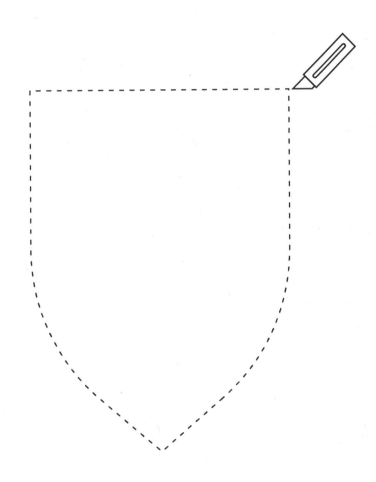

"Letters from the Battlefield"
Teen Contributor Bios

Special thanks to the following teens who have been active on the spiritual battlefield and who have been brave enough to share their stories with us. Their "Letters from the Battlefield" are a vulnerable glimpse into what it means to engage in the spiritual battle as a teen in today's world. I pray each reader is touched and inspired by the vulnerability of these young men and women and that their words of wisdom give others the courage to heed the call to battle and equip themselves with the armor of God.

Madison Billingsley attends high school in Austin, Texas. She has a heart for missions and has served Syrian refugees in Athens, Greece, over the past three summers. She loves to write, sing, and spend time with her friends and family.

Ashley Bird is Catherine and Travis Bird's oldest daughter. She is currently studying Allied Health at Texas A&M University in the hopes of pursuing a career as a Physician Assistant. Ashley is passiontate about missions and volunteering in her community, but she also enjoys spending time with her family and friends and exploring her new home in Aggieland.

Emma Kathryn Bird, or EK as she is commonly known by her family and friends, is Travis and Catherine Bird's youngest daughter. As a natural encourager and with a heart for serving others, EK immensely enjoys volunteering within her community and church. She spends most of her time focused on her studies, practicing on her year-round competitive swim team, and dreaming up ideas for her future Etsy store. When EK has downtime, however, she is mostly found reading, writing, crafting, or spending time with her friends.

Andrew Bleakley will graduate high school in June 2021 and plans to attend college, where he will pursue his interests in math, science, and computers. In his free time, he enjoys playing guitar, volunteering at the food bank, spending time with friends and family, and playing video games. He lives with his family in Raleigh, North Carolina.

Breck Echelberger is from Austin, Texas, where he is currently a junior in high school. He is a hip-hop DJ known as *DJ Breck* and has shared his musical talents at high school dances and corporate parties. Breck produces his own music and aspires to work with top artists such as Lecrae. In his spare time, he teaches guitar and piano and is the lead bassist in his band, Church Revival. Follow Breck on Instagram @breckelberger.

Baylee Ewing is a sophomore at the University of Louisiana at Monroe (TALONS OUT!). She is majoring in graphic design and enjoys drawing, reading and listening to music in her spare time. She loves traveling with her family, Bird crew included, as it is always an adventure! Baylee enjoys serving her community and being involved with retreats with her fellow youth group team and friends. As a book lover, she is in awe of her Aunt Cat.

Abby Ferguson is a native Texan and a junior in high school. She dances competitively while also staying active and serving in preschool, middle school, and high school environments at her church. Abby is the niece of Catherine and Travis Bird and the daughter of Craig and Jen Ferguson. In her spare time, she loves spending time with friends and family and working on orders for her crewneck sweatshirt business, "Crewnecks by Abby." Abby hopes to go to Juja, Kenya, with her church this coming summer to serve at Fountain of Life church and the families and orphans they support.

Ethan Fritz is a native-born Texan and lives with his parents and younger brother in Georgetown, Texas. He is currently a sophomore in high school who loves playing basketball on his homeschool team, the Round Rock Raiders. Ethan is an active member of his church, attending youth group, serving in the kids' ministry, and working on the Tech Team. In his spare time, he loves playing video games, airsoft, board games, reading, and having fun with his friends.

Hayden Jackson is a freshman at Ouachita Baptist University. He is the son of Brent and Annika Jackson, and he has four siblings: Sara, Seth, Zane, and Grace. The two most important things for Hayden are the Lord and his family, but he enjoys a variety of activities, including country music and a good two-step.

Abby Justice is a senior in high school who loves to sing in the choir and is very involved in her church. She enjoys going on mission trips to share God's love by assisting people who need it most. Abby plans to major in music education when she attends college, so that she can share her passion for music with future students as their choir director.

Emily Mazar attends Abilene Christian University and has known the Bird family since childhood. She loves Jesus, her family, music, and dogs—in that order. She hopes her time spent in college will help her grow in herself and contribute to a community in which she can grow in Jesus, too. Her current studies are focused on English with a specialization in literature and film.

Jacob McDaniel is proud to call himself a native Texan who loves God deeply. He is an active member of his church's youth group, as well as an athlete on a competitive year-round swim team. When he has free time, he enjoys gaming with his friends and family, both online and with old-school tabletop games. Jacob is a high school student who enjoys the freedom of homeschooling. He lives with his parents, younger brother, and dog.

Juliana (Juju) Murillo is currently studying Public Health at the University of Texas at Austin in hopes of one day being able to provide medical care in underdeveloped countries. In her free time, she loves listening to good music, laughing with her friends, and consuming way too much Red Bull.

Victoria Murphey is currently majoring in Biological Sciences at Clemson University with hopes of becoming a Physician Assistant. She loves Jesus, cheering on her Tigers, playing volleyball, spending time outdoors, and singing praises to the Lord.

Paige Patel is a proud half-Indian, half-Polish sixteen-year-old who repented from her sins and accepted Christ as her Lord and Savior when she was seven, and he has been so, so good to her. She loves crafting things, and her hobbies include hiking, exploring the woods, dachshund and chicken wrangling, trap shotgun shooting, reading, crochet, beading, painting, sketching, and gardening—most of which lie in unfinished projects on the shelves in her room. She has also been attempting to teach herself how to whittle with allegedly disastrous results, according to her sisters and parents. She disagrees and thinks a horrendously scarred block of wood totally looks like a mermaid.

Abigail Woodall is eighteen years old and lives in Texas. She loves listening to music every chance she gets, painting, and doing pretty much anything that involves the outdoors. She considers her parents to be her best friends, along with a girl who is the sister of her heart. Abigail embraces Jesus with all she is and wants to share the love of God with everyone she can.

About the Author

Catherine Bird is a Bible study teacher and author who is passionate about fostering families of faith by helping parents and tweens explore the wonder of God's Word. She has written several books, including *Becoming a Girl of Grace: A Bible Study for Tween Girls and Their Moms*, *Building Circles of Grace: A Bible Study for Tween Girls and Their Moms*, and *The Art of Amen*. Cat's messages equip and encourage families to

- Break out of society's mold of "normal" and embrace the authentically created people God designed each of us to be.
- Embrace the Truth that each and every person bears the image of our Creator and was created with purpose for a purpose.
- Join the counterculture of other parents, tweens, and teens who no longer feel conformed to worldly expectations.
- Find release from busy schedules and be transformed by spending time in God's Word together.

When she is not writing, Catherine spends a great deal of time with family and friends. Being a wife and mama fuels her heart, and making memories with her people rates high on her list of priorities. She also enjoys anything that has to do with colored pencils, glitter, and glue. Catherine likes to say she is multilingual, and crafting is definitely a language she speaks well. When she needs to press pause on the busy rhythm of daily life, she is often found on a hiking trail, enjoying nature in some way, or curled up with her hubby on their patio. She is also a proud graduate of Texas A&M University (Whoop!).